CAREERS
IN WRITING

VGM Professional Careers Series

CAREERS
IN WRITING

BLYTHE CAMENSON

VGM Career Books
NTC/Contemporary Publishing Group

Library of Congress Cataloging-in-Publication Data

Camenson, Blythe.
    Careers in writing / Blythe Camenson.
        p. cm. — (VGM professional careers series)
    Includes bibliographical references.
    ISBN 0-658-00103-5 — ISBN 0-658-00104-3 (pbk.)
    1. Authorship—Vocational guidance   I. Title.   II. Series.
PN151.C279   2001
808´.02—dc21   00-44214
                                    CIP

Published by VGM Career Books
A division of NTC/Contemporary Publishing Group, Inc.
4255 West Touhy Avenue, Lincolnwood (Chicago), Illinois 60712-1975 U.S.A.
Copyright © 2001 by NTC/Contemporary Publishing Group, Inc.
All rights reserved. No part of this book may be reproduced, stored in a retrieval
system, or transmitted in any form or by any means, electronic, mechanical,
photocopying, recording, or otherwise, without the prior written permission of
NTC/Contemporary Publishing Group, Inc.
Printed in the United States of America
International Standard Book Number: 0-658-00103-5 (hardcover)
                                           0-658-00104-3 (paperback)

01 02 03 04 05 06 HP 19 18 17 16 15 14 13 12 11 10 9 8 7 6 5 4 3 2 1

CONTENTS

The tools of the trade. Sample query letter. The elements of a screenplay. The making of a Hollywood film. What the studios look for. Where big-studio execs get their material. Film festivals. Contacts. Is there hope? An alternative to the big guys. Do you need an agent? The money you'll earn. First-hand account. Final words of advice.

Good technical writing should not be an oxymoron. Making a name for yourself. Job titles. Technical writing fields. Where technical writers work. Technical editors. Job outlook. The training you'll need. Courses in technical writing. The money you'll earn. The job hunt. First-hand accounts. Final words of advice.

Marketing and advertising. Job titles. Public relations. In-house or freelance. Possible employers. The training you'll need. Career outlook. The job hunt. The money you'll earn. First-hand accounts. Final words of advice.

Agent. Book reviewer. Comedy writer. Contest judge. Copyeditor. Critiquer. Ghostwriter. Greeting card writer. Newsletter writer. Reader. Resume writer. Speechwriter. Writing instructor/lecturer. The money you'll earn. First-hand accounts. Final words of advice.

ABOUT THE AUTHOR

Blythe Camenson is a full-time writer with more than four dozen books and numerous articles to her credit, including *Your Novel Proposal: From Creation to Contract* (Writer's Digest Books), which she coauthored with Marshall J. Cook.

As director of Fiction Writer's Connection (www.fictionwriters.com), a membership organization for new writers, she edits and writes for *Fiction Writer's Guideline* (the FWC newsletter), provides a free critiquing service to members, teaches E-mail courses on how to write and get published, and speaks at various writers conferences and workshops.

ACKNOWLEDGMENTS

I would like to thank the following professionals for providing advice and career information:

Linda Addison, Poet

Marjorie Braman, Editor

Ginger Buchanan, Editor

Joan Camenson, Advertising Copywriter

Kent Carroll, Carroll and Graf

Suzanne Casey, Freelance Reporter and Stringer

Julie Castiglia, Literary Agent

Jane Chelius, Literary Agent

Rob Cohen, Literary Agent

Jim Cochran, Technical Writer/Producer/Director

Susan Ditz, Public Relations Writer

Elizabeth English, Screenwriter

Paula Eykelhof, Editor

Kathleen Frost, Documentation Specialist

Russell Galen, Literary Agent

Laura Anne Gilman, Editor

Jan Goldberg, Nonfiction Book Writer

Marcus Grimm, Radio Copywriter

Rod Stafford Hagwood, Fashion Writer/Editor

Christina Hamlett, Screenwriter

Joseph Hayes, Freelance Writer

Martha Hollis, Nonfiction Book Writer

Susan Isaacs, Novelist

Barbara Karst-Sabin, Technical Writer

Anne Marie King-Jakubiak, Reporter

Frances Kuffel, Literary Agent

Tanya Lochridge, Freelance Medical/Health Care Writer

Nancy Love, Literary Agent

Newman Mallon, Public Relations Writer

Bob Mansker, Deputy Public Printer of the United States

Evan Marshall, Literary Agent

Wendy McCurdy, Editor

Linda B. Morelli, Novelist

George Nicholson, Literary Agent

Lori Perkins, Literary Agent

Clay Reynolds, Novelist

Marina Richards, Advertising/Marketing Writer

Pesha Rubenstein, Literary Agent

Peter Rubie, Literary Agent

Anne Savarese, Former Editor

John Scognamiglio, Editor

Michael Seidman, Editor

Judith Smith-Levin, Novelist

Carma Spence-Pothitt, Newsletter Writer

Barbara Stahura, Freelance Writer

Polly Starnes, Media Relations Consultant/Speechwriter

Karen Taylor Richman, Editor

Cherry Weiner, Literary Agent

Nancy Yost, Literary Agent

Susan Zeckendorf, Literary Agent

CAREERS
IN WRITING

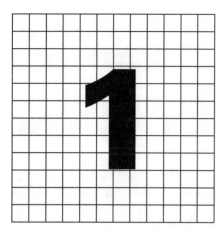

THE WRITER'S LIFE

Although writers come from all sorts of backgrounds and differ from one person to the next, they do share a few things in common. Writers love words. They love how they sound and feel and how they fit together in original and rhythmic ways.

They love playing with an idea and letting it grow until it becomes a workable article, advertisement, story, novel, or nonfiction book.

They love seeing the words fill up their computer screen and print out in neat lines on what was once a blank sheet of paper.

They love the sense of accomplishment they feel when a project has been completed, when it satisfies a client, or when it finds a home in a book or magazine.

They love seeing their name in print, giving them credit for their writing, and they love receiving the check, which in essence says, "Thanks for a job well done."

However, they have frustrations and disappointments, too. Becoming a professional writer is not an easy task. The new writer faces stiff competition from experienced writers with proven track records. Impersonal rejection slips become a way of life, and new writers must wonder at times if they have a better shot at winning the lottery than at getting published.

But new writers do get published every year—more often than lottery hopefuls win big money prizes. It takes a lot of persistence and a little luck, but if it's what you want more than anything else, you *can* make it happen.

Becoming a published, career writer has only one thing in common with a lottery—you have to buy a ticket to win. You have to write and submit your work in order to get published.

Some new writers get stalled early on, before their careers even get a chance to take off. They write and write but are reluctant to send their work in. The problem boils down to fear of rejection. But rejection is the name of the game. Even professional writers get turned down occasionally. But savvy writers let rejections guide them rather than stymie them. A rejection means you took the chance and submitted your work for approval—and that's a big first step. You should congratulate yourself.

Rejection could also mean that the work you submitted was not right for that particular editor or agent, for that particular publishing house or publication. Nothing more, nothing less. Let the rejection encourage you to revise your work or retarget the markets to which you submit it.

Rejection isn't the only adversity writers face.

Self-employed writers work alone and can often feel isolated—until the phone rings, that is, and a friend wants to chat. Often friends and family don't understand that, although you work at home, you do indeed have a real job and can't take off work at a moment's notice.

Writers must also cope with irregular paychecks and financial insecurity, at least until they are established. But even then, writers can't be sure how often a check will arrive and how many checks there will be each year. (And if you mention your concerns to certain people, you might be told the solution is easy: go out and get yourself a "real" job!)

But writing *is* a real job. Writers facing deadlines put in more hours than their 9-to-5 friends. They work days, nights, weekends, holidays. Ask writers the last time they took a vacation, and they might stare blankly at you. Although writers can usually boast a more than adequate vocabulary, *vacation* is just not one of the words on the list.

Successful writers are disciplined, even driven. They are multitaskers, able to set priorities and meet deadlines, whether from an editor or self-imposed. Most writers feel that writing isn't even a choice; it's something they are compelled to do, just as something compelled you to pick up this book.

In the pages ahead you will learn about all the different writing careers and how you can get started. You will meet some successful writers and find out what helped them. (Note that though most have college degrees—with majors ranging from math to computers—their educational backgrounds aren't featured. For the most part, formal university degree programs don't guide students toward professional writing careers.)

In the appendixes you will find valuable resources that will help you on your way, including contact information for professional associations, a listing of courses that *will* put you on the track toward publication, and a list of useful reference and how-to books. As much as successful writers love to write, they also love to read—and they know that reading about writing is an important part of the process.

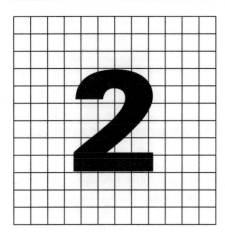

WRITING FICTION

"There are three rules for writing the novel. Unfortunately, no one knows what they are."

—W. Somerset Maugham

"Writing a novel is a terrible experience, during which the hair often falls out and the teeth decay."

—Flannery O'Connor

Let's be honest. The fiction-writing arena is the most difficult area in which to establish a career for yourself. It might take quite a while to break in, even to get just one novel published. Markets for short stories have shrunk over the years, and unless your name is Robert Frost or Maya Angelou, chances are you won't be writing "poet" as your profession on your tax returns.

If your goal is to see your name not only on a glitzy book jacket but also somewhere in the top ten on bestseller lists, remember there are only a few slots and millions of writers with the same aspirations as you.

Having said that, with writing ability—or the willingness to learn—an understanding of how the marketplace works, and a great deal of persistence, getting your fiction published is not impossible. A lucky few might even make it big. Stephen King had to start somewhere. His first novel, *Carrie*, was rejected dozens of times before it found a home. Let's look at what's involved.

CREATING A SALABLE PRODUCT

As in any industry, if you are going to sell something, you must have a quality product the public wants to buy. How you go about creating that product will, in part, determine how successful you'll be.

To create a marketable product, in this case a salable manuscript, you need to follow these five steps. Although they may seem obvious, many new writers ignore them.

FIVE STEPS TO A SALABLE PRODUCT

Step 1: Read Before You Write

Before you sit down to write, agents and editors will advise you to read other writers. Read for style, read for content, read for technique. Read to understand the marketplace and to determine if what you want to write will fit in.

"The best advice I can give," says agent Nancy Yost of Lowenstein Associates, "is read, read, and read some more. It's important to read other writers and to know what other people are reading. The best writers are avid readers."

Reading other people's work will give you a more in depth understanding of the marketplace, and it will help you improve your own writing as well.

"I like books that show me that the writer has read outside his genre," says Ginger Buchanan, senior executive editor with the Berkley Publishing Group.

Executive editor Kent Carroll says, "Take a book you like and go through it a second time. Dissect it, take it apart to see how the thing is structured, what the convention of storytelling is. Pay particular attention to how the book is organized. I think you can learn a lot from that. But don't just imitate it. Let it come from your own heart, your own mind, your own imagination."

"Read a lot, but not just the established writers, such as Danielle Steel or Stephen King," advises agent Pesha Rubenstein. "Read everything current, the new authors that are being put out now. This is the kind of material that publishers are looking for."

Karen Taylor Richman, an editor at Silhouette, gives the same advice. "*Read! Read! Read!* The one thing an author and editor have in common is their love for words. Knowing your market, understanding where you're sending your manuscript and why you feel a certain house is the one for your book, is probably the most important homework a person can do. Remember, everything you're seeing out on the shelves now was bought a while ago, so something you are sure is a new idea or a fresh twist may not be. The key is to be professional about it. And if you want to write for Silhouette, you should be reading Silhouette books to get a feel for what we're looking for."

Walker and Company mystery editor Michael Seidman advises, "Read fiction, all kinds of fiction. I've found that reading bestsellers is a frustrating experience, because no one can tell you why a particular book made it in spite of everything that's wrong with it. But, if nothing else, it will reaffirm for you the fact that sometimes God smiles, and why shouldn't that smile grace you?"

Marjorie Braman, publishing director at HarperPaperbacks, sums it up nicely. "If you want to be a writer, the best thing you can do for yourself, for a number of reasons, is to read a lot. There's the commercial reason of knowing what's working and how to tailor your book for a specific audience. And also, if you read voraciously, it opens you up to a broader approach in your own writing. You can hone your skills by reading people who are good writers."

Afraid to read for fear your writing will be adversely affected? Some writers make that excuse for not reading. Don't be one of them. This mind-set can sabotage new writers. Nancy Bereano, editor at Firebrand, says, "When writers say to me, 'Oh, I never read anyone else because I don't want to be influenced by them,' I laugh hysterically. Give me a break."

Step 2: Write for the Market

Editors and agents want you to be aware of the market and to write for it. Without a commercial product, they would have nothing to sell.

New writers often sit down and try to write something first, and then think about selling it, without really knowing the market. But you've got to write to the market. If you are writing a romance, you have to understand romance novels. If you are writing science fiction, you have to have a good idea of what is already on the shelves and what people are buying. And if you want to have your book considered by a particular publisher, become familiar with that publisher's list.

"Remember, you need to sell yourself to an agent or an editor," says Berkley editor Ginger Buchanan, "and you won't have a lot of success if you are just stumbling around in a vacuum. Read *Publisher's Weekly*. Read magazines on the genre you are interested in. Study the markets so you know what is happening. It's basic, but you won't get anywhere without paying attention to those types of details. Later, you can rely on your agent to keep track of markets and trends, but beginning writers really have to know what the business is doing. If you don't work hard at the business end of your writing, you're just dooming yourself to disappointment."

Says Peter Rubie, an associate with Perkins, Rabiner, Rubie & Associates Literary Agency, "I'm not out there to say no, although people have that impression about agents. But the reality is that the bulk of material agents receive is just not up to a publishable standard. I love to come across great material, but people don't read enough and have no idea what's fresh and what isn't, what's been done or what hasn't. I get queries that say, 'I've written a unique book about a vampire that's called AIDS.' It seems like a great idea except that I get the same idea sent to me at least ten times a week."

Agent Nancy Love explains: "Be sure you know who your audience is. Know where your writing fits. Read a lot of the same type of books you are writing, and follow the rules for that type."

Step 3: Write for Yourself

Step 3 sounds as if it contradicts the advice in Step 2, but it really doesn't. Writing for the market and writing for yourself can coexist. Market-savvy writers understand the fine line here and know how to blend both elements.

Agent Russell Galen of Scovil, Chichak, Galen Literary Agency, Inc. has this to say: "The writing process should be shaped internally, by the writer himself, not by me or by the marketplace. It isn't simply that this makes for better books, though of course it does; it actually makes for more commercial books. When the writing process is shaped externally, the result is always an obvious knockoff, an ersatz Rolex made in Hong Kong, and I can spot it."

"Write what you love to read," says agent Cherry Weiner. "All too often writers will say that they really love such and such a genre, but they will never get in, so they are going to write something else because it's easier. Nothing is easy to write. If you don't love the genre you are writing in, it will show and you won't make it."

"I think writers should write what they like," says John Scognamiglio, senior editor at Zebra Books. "I don't think a writer should decide to write a historical romance just because that's what's selling now. They need to combine what they like to read or write with what's selling."

Says Anne Savarese, former editor at St. Martin's Press, "It's easier to sell a first novel if it fits into some kind of genre. But often writers worry too much about tailoring their work to what they think publishers want. Even to the point of what kind of novel they're going to write. I think it's best to be true to what you want to do. If you have a novel in mind, you should write that novel as well as you can. Certainly you want to send it to a publisher who will most likely be interested in it, but sometimes, for example, new writers will say, 'Oh, these techno-thrillers are really big, why don't I write one of those?' But that's usually not a good idea. If you're not writing something you're really interested in, or know well, it's going to show."

Paula Eykelhof, senior editor at Harlequin Toronto, says, "Write the story that's close to your heart. Are you drawn to stories of strong, risk-taking women, stories with adventure, stories that feature family drama? Write what you want to read—and do it in your own way."

"Don't try to fake it," agent Evan Marshall advises. "Write only the kind of books you love to read and never deviate from that. Find your niche and stay in it and believe in yourself. Don't leave it just because you get rejected. If you're really good, you will be published."

Agent Jane Chelius says, "Don't worry about the market, where you think the market is, where you think the market is going. The market is very, very tough. I think you have to write your own book. You might as well write the book that's your heart's desire, because it's too hard to psych out the market. You know, we're seeing some very unusual, quirky things work really well."

Step 4: Learn How to Write

This seems like such an obvious step, you might be wondering why it's even included. But it's a step many new writers often overlook. You might have been reading avidly all your life and feel more than ready. And yes, reading other writers does help with your own writing. But it's often not enough to bring your work up to publishable standards.

Let's compare an aspiring writer with an aspiring physician. It's true that part of the training for a medical student is to observe seasoned doctors at work. But before students are even allowed in a hospital room or an operating theater, they must sit in lecture halls, read and absorb countless textbooks, and study, study, study.

Can you imagine a med student being shown on the first day an operating table with a tray of instruments next to it—and being told to begin a surgical procedure? Hardly.

Learning how to write is not something that happens in a day or in a vacuum. Yes, being an avid reader is an important part of the process, but it is a process—an ongoing process—and there are other elements to consider.

Here are some avenues to pursue to learn the craft of writing.

How-To Books. In addition to your mainstream or genre reading, don't forget the textbooks of the trade. Hundreds of how-to books for writers are available on every aspect of writing the novel. They cover writing in general and narrow in on specific topics. Want more insight into plot, dialogue, characterization, voice, style, viewpoint, action, and conflict? A book out there covers it.

There are books on grammar, too. You've probably heard about this or that famous writer who couldn't spell or whose grammar would have horrified his seventh-grade English teacher. That's what editors are for, right?

Wrong. In today's market that writer would have a difficult time getting his or work considered seriously, never mind published. Of course, an agent or editor might overlook the glaring mistakes. But the story and characters would have to be pretty outstanding to keep their attention beyond the first paragraph. Why lower your chances?

Magazines and Newsletters. In addition to how-to books, there are very good periodicals to help you. *Writer's Digest* magazine, *The Writer*, and countless newsletters put out by various writers associations are all good sources from which to glean information.

University Writing Programs. Many new writers pursue a master's degree in writing, and for some this is an excellent way to hone skills. But professionals—authors, agents, and editors—have mixed feelings about these programs. Editor Michael Seidman says, "I think they can be brilliant training grounds, but too many of them are insular and wind up teaching you how to teach a master's course.

"But, they can serve to stretch your imagination and force you to look at writing from perspectives that might not be your usual ones. So, in the end, if you have the time and finances to attend, I'd go for it."

Bestselling author Susan Isaacs is glad she didn't attend a writing program. "If I had taken a writing class, I would surely have lost [my own writing voice] and come out writing present tense fiction like everyone else in New York."

Adult Education Programs. While there might be a bit of snobbery attached—for and against attending a graduate-level course in creative writing—many fine adult-education programs offer workshops, seminars, and classes taught by solid, experienced writers and teachers.

Writers Conferences. Writers conferences are another good vehicle for learning how to write. While excellent for networking—meeting agents, editors, and other writers—they also afford you the opportunity to hear successful authors speak on novel-writing techniques.

Agent Julie Castiglia agrees that a new writer must invest some time, money, and energy in learning the craft. "People just have an idea or write a book out of nowhere and then look for an agent. They think they can tackle a book without spending any money or effort on training. They expect their book to be top-notch without going to writers conferences, taking classes, or learning the craft of writing. Even if you are very talented, you need instruction and networking in order to develop your writing to the fullest potential. If you haven't invested yourself in learning to write, you are wasting your time seeking an agent."

For starting writers, writers conferences are beneficial, especially in some of the genre areas. Romance, mystery, and science fiction have many writers conferences, and they are useful not only for educational purposes, but also for moral support. They give you a sense that you are not alone.

Support Groups. Many writers depend on critique or support groups. A well-chosen group with a particular focus and a set of guidelines to follow can provide valuable feedback on your work.

Editor John Scognamiglio says, "You should always try to get someone to read your work. A lot of times writers can't distance themselves enough, and someone else might find something you might have missed. Some writers belong to a critique group or have a writing partner. A writer shouldn't be afraid of criticism; part of writing is rejection. It's just a matter of building a tough shell and knowing what your strengths and weaknesses are."

Agent George Nicholson of Sterling Lord Literistic says, "I think it is important to belong to a writers group, but it is also important to be your own person. Too many novice writers are uncertain about their skills and pay too much attention to what others say. While it is important to listen to what others say, trust in your own instincts and judgment."

Critiques. Paid critiquing by a trusted professional is another possibility to consider. The critiquer's comments can help pinpoint your problem areas and offer suggestions on how to correct them.

Think back to our earlier example of doctors learning their profession. Considering the investment of both time and money that a doctor has to make to pursue a medical career, writers have it easy. A few how-to books, some market guides, a well-chosen conference or two a year, perhaps a manuscript critique, all add up to a small amount of money, comparatively speaking, and it is money well spent.

As agent Evan Marshall says, "Before you even approach an agent, learn your market inside out and master the techniques of your craft the best you can."

Step 5: Polish Your Product

Many new writers are so excited about the prospect of seeing their name in print, they rush too quickly to place their material in the hands of agents and acquisitions editors. Typing "The End" on that last page isn't necessarily your signal to get the mailers and SASEs (self-addressed, stamped envelopes) ready.

Yes, it's cause for celebration. Many people will tell you they have a great book in them. But only a small percentage actually sit down and write that book. You're one of a select few who applied bottom to chair and produced a finished product.

But is it really finished? Your product might not be ready for the marketplace. In the rush to publish, many new writers inadvertently defeat their efforts. They send out their first draft instead of their tenth. They send out sloppily prepared manuscripts. They send out novels with grammatical errors and typos. They send out short stories with point of view problems, plotting problems, characterization problems, and loose ends galore.

"I really believe in writers rewriting their material," says editor John Scognamiglio. "When someone sends something off it should be really polished. Writers learn a lot when they go over their material. I think you can get better if you keep working at it."

Agents and editors receive countless submissions, and most of those are rejected. Some submissions are inappropriate—they have been mistargeted, sent to the wrong house or agency. Others shriek of amateur writing or offer tired story lines.

Editors and agents can easily spot first-novel problems. If you learn how to spot those problems in your own work *before* sending it out, you'll be giving yourself an edge against the competition.

FIRST-NOVEL PROBLEMS

Listen to what the experts say. Here several agents and editors comment on what they consider to be deal-breakers, sure guarantees of a rejection letter finding its way into your SASE.

Plot

Evan Marshall, Literary Agent, Evan Marshall Literary Agency: "I get novels where it looks as if someone just sat down and started typing without any overall plan—didn't think about who would be the best viewpoint character, for example. I've seen every possible kind of craziness: books told completely in summary, novels all in narration or all in dialogue.

"Not paying attention to plot is like saying you want to paint, but you don't know how to open the tubes. Plot is not just a series of events worming their way around. Everything has to grow organically from what happened before it."

The Hook

Marjorie Braman, Editor, HarperCollins: "Often new writers don't understand how important the first part of the book is. The success of the first half of the book is, in some ways, more important than the success of the second half of the book. The opening scene is especially important. It's not the place to establish plot or setting. The first scene or the first chapter is the place to draw readers in and get them hooked. There are a number of different ways to do it, but too often I see too much effort going into setting up the book in the first chapter. That's not what a first chapter is for."

Wendy McCurdy, Editor, Bantam Books: "It can't just be another formula story, no matter how well done. That's just not going to be good enough. I am looking for something with a real hook, something for which I can visualize the niche it's going to reach."

Ginger Buchanan, Editor, The Berkley Publishing Group: "By far the biggest problem I encounter when reading manuscripts by new writers is a thinness of imagination. I receive plenty of perfectly well written books that have nothing original to say, because the writers read only books that are exactly like the ones they are trying to write."

Pace

Russell Galen, Literary Agent, Scovil, Chichak, Galen Literary Agency, Inc.: "Timing, pacing, rhythm. Inexperienced writers often neglect to put themselves in the reader's shoes and envision for themselves what the reading experience will be like, and as a result, their books are often paced in a way that isn't as enjoyable for the reader as it should be. Most commonly, this shows itself in pacing that is too slow, scenes that drag on, revelations that take forever to come, and when they finally come, it's too late and we've lost patience and interest.

"New writers often have trouble balancing all the different elements of the story. It has to move along at a pace the reader won't lose patience with. Sometimes I get the sense that the writer is having such a good time creating the set-up, he forgets about the book as a whole."

Narrative Tension

Susan Zeckendorf, LiteraryAgent, Susan Zeckendorf Literary Assoc. Inc.: "Another problem, which is especially true of mysteries and thrillers, is that there isn't enough suspense or narrative tension. There needs to be something to make the reader want to keep turning the pages."

Anne Savarese, former Editor, St. Martin's: "Often books can be very well written, but they are just not compelling enough. A lot of books we see are competent but not so good we think we have to publish them. Those are more problematic—there's no one thing that's specifically wrong. It just doesn't raise the temperature of the editor who's reading it to make him take the next step. And it's harder to really define why that happens. It just doesn't grab you, or it grabs you a little but not enough, or it seems derivative, just like ten other novels you've read that year. The mark of skillful writers is that their work stands out."

Storytelling

Laura Anne Gilman, Editor, Dutton: "A writer may have a good story and may write well but won't know how to tell the story. Sometimes the story isn't developed properly. There may be only 70,000 to 80,000 words written, but the story could be expanded to develop it better. Or the opposite can happen, that too much is told. A writer may put everything in from the research, while only some of it is needed for flavor and accuracy."

Michael Seidman, Editor, Walker and Company: "A good book is a combination of factors, all of which lead back to the same point—storytelling. If a writer is aware that storytelling is an extension of an oral tradition, if there's a distinctive voice, if something's happening that makes a difference in the reader's life, if there are characters you can believe in and care about who speak the way people speak, that's all that counts."

Peter Rubie, Literary Agent, Perkins, Rabiner, Rubie & Associates Literary Agency: "A lot of people come up with a good idea, but they don't know how to tell the story. But you could take a fairly mundane idea and if you tell it well enough, you can probably get it published."

Characters

Marjorie Braman: "Any time I like a character immediately or want to know more about him or her, then the author has done the job of at least attracting my attention. I'm always drawn in by character and less by plot. As an editor, plot is something I can help with suggestions about, but character and the emotional content of a book are something I can't teach. It's something that's either natural or not, so if authors have that, they've won a big battle."

Susan Zeckendorf: "Sometimes characters are not particularly original or well-developed. They should be described, not just in narrative but through their actions and dialogue. And if too many characters are introduced up front, it's difficult to remember who they all are."

Rob Cohen, Literary Agent, The Cohen Agency: "If I have a wonderful character, other shortcomings are less important to me. For a lot of agents, though, it's the writing or the actual plot. What kind of character do I find exciting? One that is unique, unusual, or just a lot of fun, and one that I can identify with."

Nancy Love, Literary Agent, The Nancy Love Literary Agency: "The thing that hooks me right off in a novel is the characters. Characters are the beginning of a book. If I don't care about the characters, I will reject it right away."

Dialogue

Evan Marshall: "Dialogue is another trouble spot. It's stiff and unrealistic or it doesn't get us anywhere. Dialogue should pretend that it's imitating life, but it doesn't really. It isn't supposed to have the incidental inconsequentials we say everyday like 'Hi, how are you?'"

Marjorie Braman: "I think that dialogue can be difficult, and in order to write realistic dialogue, you have to have a good ear. All you really have to do, of course, is listen to people around you—to strangers, to friends, and to family. But somehow, when it gets put down on paper, especially by a first-time novelist, it tends to turn rather unrealistic. An ear for good dialogue is something I think must come with time, but it should be paid attention to."

Cherry Weiner, Literary Agent, Cherry Weiner Literary Agency: "Often I see authors who are 'aspiring toward literary.' In effect, what happens is that the dialogue is stilted and formal. It doesn't sound like natural, everyday language."

The Writing Style

Evan Marshall: "The texture of the writing itself is often a problem, using too many adjectives and adverbs or giving every line of dialogue a tag with an adverb attached.

"That's amateurish. You can tell they're either not reading the books that explain what good writing is or they're not absorbing the information.

"Editors are fussier than ever, and so often I get fiction that is untrained as far as the technical aspects—viewpoint, dialogue, writing style, the misuse of adjectives and adverbs, whatever constitutes good writing as opposed to bad writing."

Laura Anne Gilman: "Good writing gets me excited. The story can be mediocre, but if you can write, I will give you the story back and tell you to send me another story. Good writing will overcome just about anything.

"Expository lumps are a turn-off! It's more than just going on and on without saying anything. It's writing for the sake of the words when there is no action. If you are reading and your eyes glaze over, or you begin skipping lines, that's an expository lump."

Nancy Love: "A lot of the novels I see need much more tightening up. The writer sends it out too soon. The manuscript could benefit from a workshop or critique group."

Content

Evan Marshall: "A lot of the books I get are about things that aren't of interest anymore—or never were. This has to do with awareness of market. For example, there are really very few KGB/CIA thrillers published anymore, but I still receive tons of them. Or books about an AIDS-like virus that's decimating the country, and some brave heroine is going to find out what laboratory is doing this. Or novels of historical fiction without a romance element set in some obscure time period in some obscure place with little interest to anyone. And no one's publishing multi-generational sagas unless you're a big name. The writer is confusing fresh ideas with out-of-the-market ideas. First be within the market and then be fresh."

Frances Kuffel, Literary Agent, Jean Naggar Literary Agency: "Too many first novels often tend to be coming-of-age novels, autobiographical in nature, about that person's experiences growing up. But the coming-of-age novel is extremely difficult to sell at this time. Several years ago the coming-of-age novel was hot. It just isn't anymore."

Voice

Marjorie Braman: "If a book is written in a voice that I don't like, that's a turnoff. For example, I'm not very fond of a humorous voice in mysteries, or one that tries too hard to be humorous.

"And an author who stands on a soapbox in a novel turns me off. Certainly, there are ways to get your point across and be entertaining at the same time, but if I feel I'm being preached to, I don't feel I'm being entertained. In fiction, the first goal is to entertain."

Viewpoint

Evan Marshall: "I advise new writers to avoid using the first person. It smacks of first novel or of gothic, and first person is difficult to sell. Some editors just don't like it. When you're just starting out, you want everything going in your favor. Why turn off three out of ten editors because of the viewpoint you've chosen?

"But the place to start thinking about this is before you begin writing. You have to decide who your viewpoint characters will be, from whose point of view the story will be told. A lot of authors don't understand the concept. That includes everything from knowing how to keep to one viewpoint in a scene, all the way to deciding who's going to be your viewpoint character.

"A multiple third-person point of view (telling the story from several main characters' point of view) is right for a bigger book with a more ambitious plot. You decide on four or five main viewpoint characters and stick to them, and you do each scene using just one of those viewpoints. You don't change viewpoints in the middle of a scene; editors shriek and grimace when they see it.

"For a smaller book, especially in certain genres, sometimes one viewpoint character is right, such as in a woman-in-jeopardy or a mystery. Use only one character's viewpoint and tell it in third person."

Background Details

Russell Galen: "Many books begin with long expositions of background, postponing until deep in the book any clear reason to keep reading. It's almost as common for a book to rush on too fast, not slowing down to lay in the necessary rich detail and background that enables characters to come alive."

Pesha Rubenstein, Literary Agent, Pesha Rubenstein Literary Agency Inc.: "A new writer often tries to present life exactly as it is, such as telling me every minute of the day or overdoing the dialogue. Things have to be true-to-life, but it can't be verbatim. Linear writing is also a problem. It's not necessary to chronicle every minute of every day in sequence. You need to jump right into the action."

Laura Anne Gilman: "Either the writer will throw in too much background material to tell what happened in the beginning, or omit so much it leaves the reader guessing. A balance has to be made, and that is difficult to do. It's not uncommon for writers to have problems with this on their second or third novels as well."

Grammar

Lori Perkins: "Clean up your grammar! It's not that most people can't write, but often new writers have terrible grammar, spelling, and punctuation. Study it and give me a high-quality manuscript."

Word Count

Laura Anne Gilman: "We use word count rather than page length because printers can vary so. A novel should be somewhere between 75,000 words and 100,000 words. Anything shorter than that isn't a novel. Longer than, say, 120,000 words is what we call a 'fat book' and becomes extremely hard to sell because the cost of printing it is so high. Mostly that length is reserved for the established or the break-out authors." [A break-out author sells much better than the publisher had anticipated, becoming a surprise bestseller. An example would be Robert Waller and his *Bridges of Madison County*. The original print run was very small.]

Frances Kuffel: "Keep it short. I have a novel right now that's pretty good, but it's 600 pages long. That will never sell because of the publisher's cost for actually producing the work. People should be thinking, How can I make this shorter? How can I make it tighter?"

SIX STEPS TO GETTING PUBLISHED

New writers learn soon enough that writing a novel is only half the battle. The other half is getting it published. How you target your submissions and how you approach editors or agents carry equal weight when producing a salable product.

Here's a step-by-step program that will help you sell your product.

Step 1: Target Your Submissions

Do your homework. Don't send a romance novel to a sci-fi publisher. Don't send a children's picture book to an agent who handles only adult fiction. Study the market guides (see Appendix B), attend conferences and meet with editors and agents face to face, talk to other writers, join professional associations geared to helping writers learn the ropes (see Appendix A).

Step 2: Craft Your Query Letter

The query letter is your first introduction to editors and agents. It's a miniproposal, with the purpose of hooking agents or editors and getting them to ask to see more. The query letter should be one page only, showcase your best writing, and avoid the mistakes many new writers make (going into too much detail, not giving enough specifics, using book-review-style copy to describe your work—save the book reviews for the book reviewers—and predicting bestseller status). Sample query letters are provided for you later in this chapter. (See Figures 2.1 and 2.2.)

Step 3: Send Them What They Want

A successful query letter will produce requests for more. The agents or editors will tell you what to send—sample chapters or the full manuscript, and possibly a synopsis. (Make sure you have enclosed an SASE—self-addressed, stamped envelope—with your query letter.) If they ask to see sample chapters, that means the first few chapters, not chapters selected randomly. And if they ask to see only sample chapters, don't be tempted to send them the entire manuscript anyway.

Step 4: Craft the Synopsis

The most successful synopses are one page, written in present tense, with your main character and his or her conflict as the focus. It's a summary of your novel's plot, written in the same style as your novel. The synopsis should feature your important plot points, but it need not cover every detail or subplot. To learn more about writing the synopsis, see Appendixes B and C.

Step 5: Submit a Professional Package

Follow these format rules when submitting your manuscript. Manuscripts should be double-spaced; query letters and synopses should be single-spaced. Right margins should not be justified. Your name, book title, and page number should be in a heading on the top of every page. You should use only white paper, with text printed on one side. Font size should be 12 with black ink in either Times New Roman or Courier. A cover page should include your name, address, phone number, E-mail address, genre, and word count. (But not the copyright symbol. It's a sign you're an amateur if you do include it.) For resources on manuscript format and the submission package see Appendix B.

Step 6: Wait

Many new writers send off their material, then begin the wait. But it can take weeks and, more often than not, months to receive a reply. And, more often than not, the reply will be a rejection. How to deal with this? Don't wait. Get busy writing your next novel, and the one after that. It's rare for a first novel to break in. If you're hard at work on your next project, rejections on your first won't feel as bad. The more manuscripts you have polished, the more hope you have. Rejection is the name of the game, and successful writers develop a thick skin to cope with it.

SAMPLE QUERY LETTERS

The query letter in Figure 2.1 landed the author an agent. The book subsequently was optioned for a TV movie. Publication is pending.

Linda B. Morelli sent her query for *Fiery Surrender* (see Figure 2.2) to nineteen agents. Below is a breakdown of agent responses:

- four agents were not taking on new clients

- six agents were not interested

- nine agents requested her synopsis/sample chapters and/or the complete manuscript

Linda sent her material to the nine who requested more. Here are the responses of those nine:

- three reported they were not taking on new clients

- four felt the book was not for them

- one was on the West Coast and felt Linda would be better served by a New York agent since they are close geographically

- one wrote back a week after receiving her manuscript and asked to represent her

Before going with this agent, Linda checked with Romance Writers of America to ensure he had no complaints against him, spoke with him on the phone, then signed with him.

In spite of Linda's precautions, she later learned through more networking and her own experiences that the agent/client relationship was not the best fit. She switched to another agent, Linda Hyatt of Hyatt Literary Agency, whom she met at a writers retreat, and she is now happily represented.

Linda reports that this particular manuscript has been edited down to 90,000 words and is now out with publishers who expressed interest to Linda's agent.

DO YOU NEED AN AGENT?

Many writers have submitted their work to publishers on their own and have gotten published. Some genre publishers, such as romance and mystery, are more than happy to look at unagented submissions. But so many of the big publishers in New York won't touch a manuscript that comes directly from the writer. They depend on agents to screen out the slush from the rest. And many editors feel more comfortable keeping finances out of their relationship with writers.

Figure 2.1 Sample Query Letter

(On letterhead with phone number and E-mail address.)

Date

Editor or Agent's Name, Title (The title isn't necessary for agents.)
Publishing House/Agency
Address

Dear Mr./Ms. Name,

Have you ever been in a new town, then thought you recognized someone from back home? It happens to all of us, imagining a familiar face in a strange environment. But when Abby Clark Trenton started seeing a Matthew Bowman look-alike everywhere she turned, it wasn't a comforting experience. San Angelo, a small coastal community in central California, was the last place she expected to find her first husband. Matthew had been killed aboard Abby's cabin cruiser the year before. He was dead, Abby was sure of it. She ought to know. She had killed him herself.

Widow is a 79,000-word woman-in-jeopardy novel that tells the story of Abby Clark Trenton, a freelance photographer who escapes an abusive marriage and tries to start her life over. She has a new job, a new husband, and a beautiful new home overlooking the ocean.

But now her worst nightmare is here, stalking her, his features slightly altered, denying his identity. Calling himself Ted Lawson, he strikes up a friendship with Abby's new husband, writer Dale Trenton, and instills himself into the Trenton household. It's a friendship Abby is sure will end in tragedy. Too many secrets and too many lies have made it impossible for Abby to confide in Dale fully. She feels powerless to stop the erosion—until she realizes what she must do.

To save herself, her husband, and her marriage, Abby must act first.

She must kill Matthew Bowman . . . yet another time.

I am a full-time writer (four dozen books to my credit) and director of Fiction Writer's Connection, a membership organization for new writers. My bio is attached.

May I send you the complete manuscript?

Sincerely,

Blythe Camenson

Figure 2.2 Sample Query Letter

Date

Agent's Name
Agency Address

Dear Agent's Name,

My historical romance, *Fiery Surrender*, tells the story of Monique von Strade, the headstrong daughter of a Prussian Count who knows from the moment she meets the enigmatic Pierre Latier that he will steal her heart as surely as he will save her honor. But love is the furthest thing from Pierre's mind. He's a man with a dark past who, under the guise of Pierre Marchant, serves King Louis XVI as a spy. Pierre can ill afford to think of anything save his upcoming mission, escorting French arms to the American Colonies.

When Pierre pays a sudden visit to her in Paris, Monique realizes the depth of the love she holds for him. Confessing her unwilling betrothal to a Comte she despises, she agrees to meet Pierre secretly. Within Pierre's passionate embrace, Monique can no longer deny the fierce, burning desires that flood her. Later, believing Pierre married her only to protect her family's honor, she resolves to win his love, even though it means following Pierre into the dangers of war.

Set against the American Revolution and the October 1781 Battle of Yorktown, Virginia, *Fiery Surrender* is a sensual story of two people who eventually face the inevitability of their love. The novel runs approximately 130,000 words and is ready for an agent's assessment. To give authenticity to my novel, I have conducted considerable research at the Library of Congress and in both Williamsburg and Yorktown, Virginia.

I have an extensive background as an editor/creative writer and am an avid reader of historical and contemporary romances. I am an active member of Washington Romance Writers, Virginia Romance Writers, and Romance Writers of America. I am currently in the final stages of completing a second novel, a category mystery romance.

If the premise of the book appeals to you, I'd be happy to send the complete manuscript.

Sincerely yours,

Linda B. Morelli

Agents have an inroad to what publishers are looking for. Good agents rarely mistarget their submissions. Having an agent gives you credibility as a writer and saves you from devoting all your time to marketing your work. With a good agent in your corner, you can devote your time to writing and know that your agent will handle the marketing and the money end of the business for you.

Of course, it's no easy feat getting an agent, but it is by no means impossible. A good query letter and an excellent novel will readily attract an agent's attention. If an agent feels he or she can sell your work, there is no reason not to take you on—whether you're new at the game or not.

The approach you would use for an agent is the same six-step process mentioned earlier in this chapter. It is not a good idea to target agents and editors at the same time, though. If you have sent your manuscript out to five or ten publishers on your own, then manage to land an agent, there will be no one left for him or her to submit to.

If you are having no luck getting an agent, you could try targeting some of the smaller publishers directly. But you might ask yourself why you aren't finding an agent. Is your query letter not sufficiently compelling? Is your manuscript not professionally crafted? Paying attention to these aspects will almost assure you an agent.

No Agent Is Better Than a Bad Agent

Just like in any industry, writers will find some unscrupulous people out there, ready to prey on their desperate desire to become published. They'll promise the world—as soon as they get the check. But the world never gets delivered.

Smart writers know that legitimate agents charge their 15 percent commission only when they sell your work to a publisher. No reading fees. No evaluation fees. No editing fees. No referrals to a book doctor with the promise of representation after you've dished out thousands of dollars and have rewritten your manuscript.

Spotting a Good Agent

When looking for an agent, target only those who are members of the Association of Authors' Representatives (AAR) (see Appendix A). AAR agents must follow a canon of ethics and are forbidden to charge fees. Agents earn their money by selling your work to publishers, not by collecting from you. You are not responsible for an agent's overhead, or cost of doing business, and don't be convinced otherwise.

Fee chargers are not the only kinds of "bad" agents out there. Most "good" agents are in New York City. While many good agents work successfully outside that arena and prejudices over out-of-town agents are dissipating, still, editors want to work with agents who have a track record. Do not be afraid to ask prospective agents who they represent and how many sales they have made.

You can expect your agent to communicate with you, to send you editor responses to your work, to negotiate the best deal for you in case of an acceptance, and to be in your corner as a truthful, hardworking advocate. If this isn't happening, it might be time to move on.

You shouldn't expect your agent to work speedy miracles for you, though. It could take an agent a year to place your manuscript—sometimes longer. If it's only been a few months and no good word has come your way, don't assume it's the agent's fault. Although you can check in with your agent occasionally, don't make frequent phone calls, expecting long conversations and hand-holding. If you keep agents on the phone too much, they won't be able to do their job—selling your manuscript.

WRITING SHORT STORIES AND POETRY

As mentioned at the beginning of this chapter, making a career for yourself writing short stories and poetry is next to impossible. Yes, you can get your work published, see your byline, and maybe even receive a small check for your efforts, but the money involved wouldn't be enough to feed your cat.

New writers often wonder if they should start with short stories as a way of breaking into the novel market. Certainly having fiction credits can help show an agent or editor that you're a professional, but each novel you submit stands on its own and is judged by its own merits. Your short story in *Reader's Digest* or *Playboy*, although wonderful clips to have, is not a guarantee of success with novels.

If writing short stories or poetry is what you love to do, then by all means go for it. But as far as making a career of it, well, there's an expression in the writing world that applies here: Don't give up your day job just yet.

THE MONEY YOU'LL EARN

Some new writers think that novel writing will make them rich and famous. But there are only ten to twelve slots on the bestseller lists, and most of those are taken up by well-known authors. In truth, the average advance for a first novel ranges from $2,500 to $5,000. Those huge million-dollar deals you hear about are not the norm. Midlist authors can make a comfortable living turning out two or three books a year, but the largest group earns less than a family would need to survive.

In most cases a writer is given an advance check upon acceptance of the manuscript—half at the onset, the other half after any required revisions are turned in. Then a royalty percentage is offered, sometimes based upon the retail price of the book, sometimes upon the net price. The royalty percentage might start at 6 percent or 8 percent, then increase with the number of copies that are sold. To receive a royalty check, though, the book first needs to earn back its advance. And sometimes that can take awhile.

With short stories and poetry, earnings can be negligible. Smaller magazines might offer just a few dollars or even just complimentary copies of the issue in which your work appears. Some of the more well-known markets, such as the *New Yorker* or *Atlantic Monthly,* pay much higher rates—one or two dollars per word—but these markets are very difficult to break into.

As with any self-employment, you, the writer, are expected to take care of your own taxes, health insurance, and any other benefits full-time workers receive.

The more you produce, the more you can earn. But remember, the time you spend marketing your work will be as much as—if not more than—the time you spend writing it.

Writing fiction is not an easy way to earn money. But if it's what you love to do, don't let that stop you. The next bestseller could be yours—you'll never know if you don't try.

FIRST-HAND ACCOUNT

Judith Smith-Levin
Mystery Writer

Judith Smith-Levin is the author of the Star Duvall mystery series. The first book, *Do Not Go Gently*, was published by HarperCollins in 1995. Books two and three, *The Hoodoo Man* and *Green Money*, and the fourth in the series, as yet untitled, are all out or under contract with Random House/Ballantine Books.

She's done other writing as well, including journalism, television newswriting, teleplays, film scripts, and theatrical plays. She also teaches courses in novel writing. (See Appendix C for universities with such courses.)

The Attraction to the Field

"I've always been a reader (since the age of three). I love words: written, read, or spoken. I love the beauty of language. Writing was the only thing I could do without trying; it just came naturally. Being published as a novelist was my dream, even while I was making a living doing other things. The attraction is that writing makes me feel good, complete. I love it.

"The genre snuck up on me. I owned a small mystery bookstore in Carmel, California, and I read everything to keep up with my customers, who were very savvy mystery people. It was then that I decided to try writing mysteries. My protagonist is a six-foot-tall, African American, female homicide lieutenant, Star-letta (Star) Duvall. As an ex–police officer, I had a lot of experiences to draw upon. Writing in the mystery genre also allowed me to humanize my officers and address some of the emotional experiences of police work."

Getting That First Book Published

"I sent my first book 'over the transom' [without agent representation] to every publisher in New York and got totally rejected. Without an agent, no one would look at it.

"So I went to the library, got a copy of *Writer's Market* and sent it to every listed agent who would read unsolicited manuscripts.

"After my blanket mailing, I decided to also send it to a 'famous' agent. Even though she wasn't listed as a 'reading' agent, my feeling was, what have I got to lose? So I sent my manuscript with a letter mentioning one of her famous clients, of whom I was a fan. In fact, I'd read the agent's name in the writer's acknowledgments. The book (my first, *Do Not Go Gently*) was read by an associate agent who liked the manuscript. The famous agent wasn't interested, but the associate eventually started her own agency and took me on as a client.

"With submissions and rejections and finally getting accepted as a client by a fledgling agent, it took a little over a year. I learned of my first acceptance from a very exuberant message left on my answering machine by the agent, followed by one from the HarperCollins editor who had purchased the book. I was stunned but happy."

Subsequent Books

"I signed a multibook contract, so the series was pretty well set. The second book in the series, *The Hoodoo Man*, was purchased from HarperCollins by Random House/Ballantine Books and became part of a new multibook deal with that company."

What the Work Is Really Like

"Since I love what I do, it's difficult to say anything negative. But writing can be a pretty tough job, mainly because you are the sole creator. Everything comes from you: characters, dialogue, plot. All of it is conceived, nurtured, and born from you. It's almost like giving birth. In addition, if you're doing a series, there's the added task of 'maturing' your characters and moving them and their lives along. It's very challenging, but I have a real sense of accomplishment at the end of my day.

"When I was just writing for pleasure, I could hang things any way I wanted, but now, I have readers and, thankfully, avid fans, who really enjoy my characters. It would be unthinkable for me to cheat them—to be lazy about the research or about the past lives and incidents that make up the characters. Continuity is very important. Do the research, do the work, and keep your characters true to themselves.

"I write at night, so my 'day' actually starts at about 8 P.M. I tend to work until about three or four in the morning. I like night work; I'm more alive after dark. Daylight is difficult for me. I have friends who suspect I might be a vampire! (There's a good story idea!)

"I get up at about 11 A.M. and do the daily things that people do. I go to the market, do laundry, clean my house, watch my soaps (yes, I love soap operas), visit with friends, and so on. The evening belongs to the work. I don't start out with an outline, just an idea. Then I sit down and do it. I'm always surprised at the way my characters take over the story. I might actually think they're going to do one thing, and they do the opposite.

"I realize that sounds a little crazy, but these people are real to me, and because they're real to me, I listen to them. That's also the key for my readers. Practically every letter I get says 'I know Star' or 'I feel I know these people.' That's a great compliment. If they aren't real to me, they won't be real to the readers, so I give them lives and voices, and I listen.

"In the second novel, *The Hoodoo Man*, my detective asks her partner if he's ever killed anyone in the line of duty. I was all set to say no, but Detective Sargeant Paresi said yes. And I was stunned. I just sat back and transcribed his experience at having had to kill someone during his first year on the street as a patrol officer. When I finished and read it back, I was amazed at the emotion. He said what it felt like to take someone's life, how painful it was for him. Even in a situation where it was kill or be killed. It was almost like being channeled. It's the most fulfilling work I can imagine.

"I don't have set hours. I work until I'm empty and then I go to bed. Usually, I turn out about twenty pages a night. I never throw anything out, because if you toss something, the next day you might realize, Hmmm, I might be able to use that.

"I work at home, in a home office that I consider a fun spot. I like toys, and so there are toys all over the place—on my computer and on my desk. There are cartoons and photos of family and people that I love. I have a great, grinning Mickey Mouse phone and a huge blowup of the Elvis postage stamp, which is framed and hanging on the wall directly in front of me. I have an Elvis clock with swiveling hips. And I have drawings and knickknacks all around, as well as my framed book covers. They provide a lot of inspiration. I also have my files and my reference books.

"My computer has a great sound system so I have lots of my favorite CDs available, and I listen to music as I work. My detective is a Motown fan, so I listen mostly to Motown music when I'm working with Star, but I also listen to a lot of blues, disco—it's happy music—and just about everything else, including lots of Eric Clapton and James Taylor."

The Upsides and Downsides

"I love that I do something that touches so many people, that my work is enjoyed by my readers. Yet, in all honesty, I'd do it even if I were the only one seeing it. And for a long time, I was!

"Doing work that I love, and meeting and hearing from people who enjoy that work, is a real upside. Readers who take the time to write or come up to me to say how much they like the books—that's a good feeling.

"What I like least are rewrites. When you're published, editors look at your work and pick it apart. That can be rough. Sometimes something you really love is cut out and that's hard. Writing is easy; rewriting is a bear!

"Writing to deadlines can sometimes be tense, especially when there's research involved in completing your story. Some writers hate doing research and actually hire other people. Since most of mine centers on the latest police techniques and the newest developments in forensics, I enjoy doing it, but it can be time-consuming. Of course, it's made easier by my having been a police officer. If I have questions, I find that my former colleagues and other police officers are always available and eager to help out."

Advice from Judith Smith-Levin

"Be prepared to work hard, and understand the financial aspects of publishing. You can have a book released and not see a penny of royalty money until six, nine, or even twelve months later. Remember that large advances have to be repaid before you start earning from the work.

"Budget your money carefully, and build your fan base. Six- and seven-figure advances go to two types of writers: authors who have a proven track record (Stephen King, Danielle Steel, Mary Higgins Clark) or celebrity tell-all books that usually disappear within weeks of their debuts, usually leaving the publishers with lots of returns and lost revenue. If you think that writing is a quick way to money and fame, you'll be disappointed.

"I personally don't believe a writer can be trained. Writing is a gift. Either you can do it or you can't. You can learn the basics of language. You can study grammar, sentence structure, spelling, and all that, but storytelling is an art, and it has to come from inside.

"The best advice of course is write what you know. Just sit down and put your thoughts on paper (or computer screen) and see where they take you. Journaling is a good way for some people to get into the habit of writing every day.

"I also believe a writer should be a reader. If you want to write romances, read them. If you want to write history, whatever, read the genre. Don't steal! But look at how things are phrased, how the dialogue works, check out the characters, see how they make you feel.

"Classic writers are also good teachers. I love to read Mark Twain. His characters and dialogue, though over a hundred years old, are still pertinent and timely. I feel the same way about Dickens. His characters are exciting and mesmerizing, even in today's world. There are also current writers who are masters at plotting, character, and dialogue.

"Bottom line: respect the work—the art—and love it, or do something else."

FIRST-HAND ACCOUNT

Clay Reynolds
Novelist

Clay Reynolds is the author of half a dozen novels in genres such as psychological suspense, crime, and historical. His titles include: *The Vigil* (Texas Tech University Press, 2000); *Agatite* (St. Martin's Press, 1986; reissued with the title *RAGE*, Signet, 1993); Pulitzer entrant *Franklin's Crossing* (Signet, 1994); *Players* (Pinnacle, 1998); *Monuments* (Texas Tech University Press, 2000); and *The Whore of Hoolian* (Berkley, 2000). He has been writing fiction professionally since 1984.

Getting Started

"I began writing fiction because I was the father of two very young children; my wife worked nights and I was sole caregiver each evening from about 4 P.M. on.

I had been working in scholarship, research, and literary criticism steadily for a number of years. My duties restricted me to the house, then, and I couldn't do the library work required for scholarship. Moreover, I had to remain awake and alert for most of an evening. Fiction writing was a way of occupying the hours after my children were down for the night.

"I completed two novels, *The Vigil* and *Agatite*. A friend of mine had been to one of those writing conferences sponsored by a writers group in Arkansas. There he obtained business cards for an agent and an editor from St. Martin's Press. I sent *The Vigil* to the agent and *Agatite* directly to St. Martin's on January 4, 1984. On January 5, 1985, the editor called me and said he had read and wanted to publish *Agatite*. I was obviously elated.

"Then I decided that this was a practical joke. I immediately telephoned St. Martin's Press in New York, asked for the editor, and to his amusement confirmed that we had just had a conversation. At the end of that second conversation, he recommended that I find an agent. I immediately telephoned the agent I had sent *The Vigil* to and left a message that I'd just sold a novel to St. Martin's Press and asked if he wanted to represent me. He phoned back within the hour and said that he hadn't had a chance to read the other book, but that he would definitely represent me. He sold *The Vigil* to St. Martin's the following week. Both books were published in 1986—January and December, respectively.

"The initial elation went away as my 'education in publishing' developed. I have since learned that publishing is a business, first and foremost. The quality of a book is the least important consideration in book acquisition and marketing. Its market appeal, demographic target, and price point are far more valuable. Publishers are operating an industry that depends on profit, and a book is a product they can sell."

Subsequent Books

"My editor at St. Martin's was replaced by someone who tentatively agreed to buy a third novel, *Franklin's Crossing*. Then she resigned to get married. The next editor reneged on the verbal promise immediately and said he would tell me what kind of novels I needed to be writing. Because he was in charge of the final editing of *Agatite*, I sat tight until it was published later in the year. The editor and I continued to have arguments about the way he was handling the books (which was not at all—he never read them, in fact) until late 1987. At that point, my first St. Martin's editor, who had become president and publisher of Dutton, agreed to buy *Franklin's Crossing*.

"It took me three years to complete the research and writing on that historical novel, *Franklin's Crossing*. I turned it in during the fall of 1990. My editor was fired two weeks later, and Dutton was absorbed by the Viking Penguin conglomerate. I had no editor for six months; then I went through a series of three editors over the next two years. Each editor wanted to make changes, significant changes, mostly cuts. With the next-to-last editor, I finally met expectations, and the novel was transmitted to galleys. The next editor demanded more changes and cuts in the galleys, all mandated to keep the price point low. The novel was issued in the spring of 1992 in hardcover, with a lurid cover that attempted to imitate Larry McMurtry's *Lonesome Dove*. Signet also agreed to reprint the paperback, mass-market editions of *Agatite* and *Franklin's Crossing*.

"To their credit, Dutton got behind *Franklin's Crossing*. They entered it into the Pulitzer Prize competition, and it won several other literary awards. They also issued a contract for a subsequent historical novel and for two crime novels.

"I finished one crime novel and submitted it, but the mood of the industry had changed. Dutton no longer wanted crime fiction or historicals. They said they were 'dead letters.' All my contracts were canceled in 1996.

"I wrote another novel, *Players*, a high-tech psychological thriller with a strong crime-novel flavor, which Carroll and Graf published in the summer of 1997. In spite of outstanding sales, they did not want another novel. They decided that crime fiction was a dead letter.

"I submitted *Monuments* to Texas Tech University Press, which has approved it for contract; they also have issued a contract to reprint *The Vigil* and *Agatite* in trade paperback editions. I am presently working on a new historical for Berkeley, titled *The Whore of Hoolian*.

"In between novels, I have also written and edited several nonfiction books and have published short fiction, poetry, original essays, and scholarly material. My most recent nonfiction book is *Twenty Questions: Answers for the Aspiring Writer*, which is based on a workshop series I have conducted over the years for writers groups and college and university programs. It was published in the winter of 1998 by Browder Springs Press.

What the Work Is Really Like

"Because I have been a university professor for all but about seven years of my writing career, I divide my time between my duties at the school and my writing. I try to arrange my schedule to allow for blocks of time to write. The administration at the University of Texas at Dallas has been most accommodating in responding to this request.

"On a writing day, I usually try to write in the mornings, but I am not at my best in the mornings. Because of my children's various activities, however, it is the best free time I have for my work. This is changing as they get older and move on with their lives. I am gradually returning to my best time, which is in the evenings.

"I now work exclusively on a word processor and computer. This facilitates my other writing and editing work, and it's a comfortable medium, although I'm not convinced it's an advantageous one in all respects. Speed and efficiency have little to do with quality work, I've discovered.

"I am never bored, but my work time is often tedious and informed by the pressure of deadlines and all the general insecurities that have to do with anything that requires inspiration and talent balanced against craft and ability.

"Writing is a solo occupation. I have little patience with people who want to talk about their work, as it bespeaks a desire to feed their egos rather than to do what that work requires, which is work. Writing is work; it's hard work, and it's exhausting if it's done right. It does not easily brook interruptions, distractions, or limitations. There is no worse enemy of mine than telephone solicitors and telemarketers.

"But my telephone is my lifeline to my agent and to other business contacts. A timely phone call can mean money in the bank; a missed call can be a disaster.

"If I'm on a roll with something, I might work eighteen to twenty-four hours straight. Writer's block is a constant and real companion. It can strike at any time, even in the middle of a sentence. Emotions in writing are very close to the surface and are often very real. They have to be generated and nurtured, but they can never override the intellect. This is hard work, and it requires a daily commitment.

"I work at home, in a home office, sheltered from television and other noises and distractions. I have a window. I take a walk from time to time. I may nap if I can't come up with an idea. I read a great deal. I spend anywhere from eight to twelve hours a day at the keyboard, often for small reward except the guarded reactions of my family. Writing is not a hobby. It can be fun—it can be marvelous fun—but it's always work, even when it's the most fun."

The Upsides and Downsides

"I like writing most when it works. There's no feeling in the world as wonderful as when things are in a groove and the words and ideas fit together in a way you know is original and you hope is profound.

"What I like next best is when I read a review or a letter from someone who has read what I've written, and the reader actually understood what I was trying to do. They don't have to like it. But if they understand it, that's the best part of the whole shooting match.

"The euphoria of seeing your words in print or seeing your books on a store's shelves fades pretty quickly; it constantly reminds you that you'd better get another book out *pdq*.

"What's most difficult is the knowledge that no matter how well you write, how good you are, or how much people like what you do, you can still fail miserably at this. We live in a consumer society; people know what they like, and they want more of it, but they want it 'new and improved,' and where writing is concerned, that's scary.

"The very worst thing about it is that no one understands what you do. No one but another writer, that is. People who read think that writing is just reading turned around backwards. They have no idea the special kind of pain that's involved or the amount of work it takes even to complete a short piece of fiction. Everyone thinks that he or she is a writer. All they need is the time to do it, they'll happily assure you. Hearing that repeated over and over is the worst thing there is.

"The second worst thing is people who complain about how much your books cost or brag that they bought one at a used book store for a third the cover price. The same people who think nothing of dropping fifty dollars on a dinner for four at a two-star restaurant whine about spending twenty bucks for a hardbound book. A writer makes zero when his or her books are bought from a used book store, remainder house, or other clearinghouse-type store—nothing. When you tell a writer you bought the book there, you have just told him that you've taken money out of his pocket."

Earnings

"From time to time, a reasonably large influx of cash comes a writer's way. A large contract can bring tens of thousands at a lump. But from this amount (which will be divided at least in half and spread over a period of six months to two years) the writer must deduct federal and state taxes, agency fees, accountant's fees, etc., to say nothing of overhead (that shiny new computer and all the updates required to keep it current with software, for example). When broken down to an hourly rate, this means that the writer makes mere cents per hour, often less.

"Rumors of huge contracts worth six figures or more are to some degree accurate. But such contracts represent less than a tenth of 1 percent of those issued. On average, a writer can expect to make between $10,000 and $20,000 from a first novel, if it's published by a major house in New York, well-publicized, and reviewed in one of the major trades. These earnings will be spread over a period of one to four years in disbursement.

Advice from Clay Reynolds

"Do not go into writing for the money. There's little of it. The best quality a writer can possess is an independent income or a job that allows you time to write.

"Be willing to spend huge amounts of time alone and learn to rely on your own judgment, opinion, and ability. Be able to take rejection (by editors, agents, the general public, your neighbors, your friends, your family, your dog) and criticism, which is always available without charge from everyone.

"Understand that writers are not celebrities, even when they are famous. They're ordinarily introverted and somewhat frumpy, ill-mannered and sour-tempered, shabby people, who probably would be happier home alone watching an old movie on the tube than talking to just about anybody.

"Be educated in the English language (if you write in English). Know the rules of the grammatical road and obey them, even when you break them deliberately. If you cannot diagram a sentence, conjugate an irregular verb, decline a personal pronoun, tell the difference between a restrictive and a nonrestrictive clause, a gerund and a participle, a linking verb and a transitive verb, you cannot be a writer. If these three sentences seem correct to you, you're not going to write effectively or successfully:

Everybody has their ticket.

A trial is different than a hearing.

She felt badly about her remark.

(Correct sentences: Everybody has his or her ticket. A trial is different from a hearing. She felt bad about her remark.)

"More advice: Read. You cannot read enough if you do nothing else for every waking minute of the rest of your life. Read, read, read. Read history, sociology, chemistry, poetry, plays, novels, short stories, quantum physics, geography, psychology, sports accounts, daily newspapers, weekly magazines, monthly journals, and high school yearbooks. Read. Especially read literature. Bestsellers only teach you what's hot, not what's good. You cannot write originally if you don't know what's been written. Then sit down and tell a story. Fiction is a lie with which we tell the truth. Tell your lie. Tell it well. But tell it as a story."

FIRST-HAND ACCOUNT

Linda Addison
Poet

By day, Linda Addison is a computer programmer, by night a poet. Her poetry and short stories have appeared in *Asimov's Science Fiction* magazine, *Dark Regions*, *Tomorrow*, *Epitaph*, *White Knuckles*, *Edgar*, *Lore*, *Pirate Writings*, *Tales of the Unanticipated*, *Haiku Headlines*, *Frogpond*, and *Brussels Sprout*. She's also currently the poetry editor for *Space & Time* magazine, a science fiction (SF)/ fantasy/horror publication. Linda has been writing for more than thirty years.

What Attracted Linda Addison to Writing

"It's more that poetry chose me. I began writing journals in high school and suddenly found myself writing poems rather than prose to explain how I felt. Before I wrote my first poem, I spent hours reading out loud to myself (Shakespeare, Edgar Allan Poe, Langston Hughes, and others). Looking back I realize that those early readings helped me recognize the music in my head as poetry.

Getting Published

"My earliest first publication was in my high school newspaper in 1969—which I don't count on my list of publications, but it was the first time I realized how much I enjoyed seeing my name in print. My first professional publication was with two poems, "Bard Wellington" and "Writing Magic," in 1994 in a magazine called *Just Write*. I had read about it in a writers market magazine called *Scavengers*. *Just Write* was a new magazine, and I had the good fortune of being published in the first issue and having a whole page myself. It was extremely exciting.

"Since then I've had more than fifty poems published and still counting. I am proudest of being published in *Asimov's Science Fiction* magazine. I've had a poem accepted each year for the last four years. But I sent my work to them for more than ten years before they started accepting my poems. This was a personal best for me because Isaac Asimov was such an influence on my writing for many years.

"To assure I continue to be published, there are two things I do regularly— write and market. I write in a journal every day. I've learned to carry a little notebook so I can jot down any interesting images or ideas that occur during the day. Experience has taught me that I can't trust my memory to bring back an interesting phrase later, but if I write a little note to myself or a few words, that usually triggers the feeling later.

"Marketing is also very important. I spend time each week checking magazines (paper and on-line) that list markets. I keep my own summaries of these markets on index cards. Each week I try to farm a new poem from my notes and journals and then list at least three or more markets for it. 'Farming' a poem means rewriting. I write most of the poems the first time on paper, but I rewrite on the computer, because it's easier to change the physical shape of the poem. I can use the computer's thesaurus to look for fresh words to replace the words I usually use. I enjoy doing something unusual with a poem I'm working on; it keeps my interest piqued, and if I don't like a poem, it will be hard to sell it to someone else.

"Finally, the big secret to getting published: I make sure I keep my poems in the mail. With a little time spent licking stamps and a lot of thick skin, I've been able to keep the acceptance letters coming.

"I'm African American, by the way, which is kind of a plus in this genre. There aren't many of us that I've met, so when I go to conventions and conferences, it's easy to get noticed and remembered. (I've been on panels for SF/horror conventions, and that's a lot of fun.)"

Writing

"I write mostly science-fiction and horror poetry. They take different creative muscles, and I enjoy both in different ways. I use my background in mathematics and science for the SF poetry, and personal reactions to negative things that happen in the world (either from my own experiences or the news) for the horror poetry.

"Since I work as a computer programmer during the day, I do the bulk of my writing in the evening (at least an hour) or while commuting back and forth to work (another hour). I like to spend a little time before bedtime writing about something from the day. Sometimes this is sparked by something interesting that someone said or something that I read.

"I use weekends to farm market the writing I've done during the week by reading through my journal or notebook for something interesting. I try to add a new poem a week to the circulating list.

"When I'm writing SF poems I like to be as scientifically accurate as possible. In general, I like to write SF poems that juxtapose hard science against human emotion. I also use the ever popular question 'What if . . .?' to come up with a different way of looking at things. For example, I was watching a special on sharks when the words 'land sharks' struck me, so I wrote a poem called "Land Sharks" about genetic engineering and what happens when it goes wrong. I sold the poem to *Asimov's Science Fiction* magazine. I've written quite a few poems after watching nature and science shows.

"Horror poems come from the dark, emotional part of my creative juices. I've actually started writing them only the last few years. I believe I needed to feel safe enough inside to face such darkness. Inspiration can begin with my own feelings of anger or fear from some memory or watching a news story. I try to invoke through images the same emotion I felt. On some level, writing out my feelings and reactions is cleansing for me.

"To keep it interesting I like to use hard images for soft emotions or vice versa. I use other tricks to make the writing different, such as writing through other points of view, as an animal or an inanimate object. I was a featured poet in *White*

Knuckles magazine, and one of the poems they printed was called "Mourning Meal." It describes in images of eating a mother's grief at the loss of her child.

"There are occasions when I'll read about a special market, such as a magazine looking for poems involving ghosts and machines, and I'll write poems just for that subject. If the magazine doesn't buy the poems, I'll find other markets for them. Anything that makes me write is a good thing."

Marketing

"I usually do marketing on the weekend, or I might take one evening during the week to read through market listings and update my cross-listings. I have an index card for each poem. I write the title and the number of lines at the top. I note possible magazine markets on the back. This is an important part of keeping circulating poems in the mail—I don't want to stop every time a poem comes back to look for the next market.

"When I send a poem out, I write the date sent and market name on the front of the card. If it comes back rejected, I write the date it came back. If the editor said anything interesting—"this poem comes close" sort of thing—I write it on the same line.

"I keep another set of index cards for markets. I write the magazine's name, address, editor's name, the kind of work they are looking for, and anything they mention about submissions (such as send poems in batches of four to ten with a maximum of fifty lines), payment, how long they say it will take to respond to submissions, and the date I found the market.

"The safest way to know if your poem will fit a market is, of course, to read a sample of the magazine, but that's not always economically feasible. However, you can read the market listings carefully and try to objectively evaluate your poems. Also, it wouldn't hurt to check out some of these magazines at bookstores that don't mind if you browse.

"I've begun to sell poems to electronic markets and paper magazines that accept E-mail submissions. This is a wonderful trend since it saves on postage, and I've found in general I get responses faster.

"Another helpful business tip is that I have a folder of printouts of the poems I'm circulating (usually two copies so I can pull one to send out and still have a copy in the folder). This is especially helpful if you have more than a handful of poems to sell. When I'm looking at a possible market, I need to reread poems to see if they could fit the guidelines.

"It's important to pay attention to how the poem is formatted on the page for submissions. This is a small and easy thing to do, but I've seen inexperienced writers make the mistake of looking inexperienced. If I'm sending four or more poems, I send them flat in a larger envelope with a smaller SASE (self-addressed, stamped envelope). I mark the poems 'disposable' so that I only have to send an SASE with one stamp on it, since having a home computer and printer makes it so easy to reprint a poem. One poem per page, name and address in the upper-right-hand corner, line count in the upper-left-hand corner."

The Upsides

"There are two things that I love about writing poetry. There is a great satisfaction that comes in letting the words flow out of me, often a healing sensation, depending on the subject. Once the poem is finished (meaning it reads well out loud) there's a magical moment when the poem is no longer connected to me and I see it as a first time reader. The images give me a chill, and I wonder where it came from; that's very enjoyable.

"The second thing I love is the most obvious: seeing a poem in print. There's something about knowing that strangers are reading it—and, I hope, getting some image from it or having a reaction, whether it's the one I had when I created it or not.

"Another thing I've enjoyed is doing poetry readings. Writing can be such a solitary process, just between the writer and the page or computer screen. Readings give me a chance to share with an audience and get reactions right away. But it can be as unnerving as it is fulfilling."

The Downsides

"To be quite honest, the only thing I don't like is the marketing part. It's necessary work, like washing dishes. If you want to eat, you've got to wash the dishes from the last meal, but few people enjoy washing dishes. I know the only way I'll see my work in print is to market, write the letters, and mail out my babies. I would gladly pay someone to do this if I could afford it."

Earnings

"The highest paying market I've been selling to is *Asimov's Science Fiction* magazine, which pays $1 a line. Often the pay is more like $5 to $10 a poem. Most magazines pay a flat rate per poem, some only a copy of the magazine. I send my poetry to the highest paying markets first, unless I have a special feeling for the magazine—perhaps they're new and I have some poems that are perfect for them.

"I don't support myself writing poetry. My income comes from computer programming."

Advice from Linda Addison

"Since the financial rewards are so hard to come by, someone who wants to be a poet has to be driven inside by the need to write poetry. I started by writing poetry and then found out some things that helped me get published:

- Keep a daily journal and carry little notebooks. Capture every image, idea, or piece of music that flows through you on a daily basis. Write all the time; don't worry about how good it is until you sit down to rewrite it.

- Read poetry. Read out loud whenever possible, especially your own poetry when you're rewriting. And keep a thesaurus nearby. Reading aloud will help you hear if you've captured the music. This is how I test whether a poem is ready to be sent out into the world.

- Do smart marketing. Don't send a cat poem to a motorcycle magazine (unless they're doing a motorcycling cat special issue). Try new magazines—they're hungry and provide a good way to get your feet wet.

- Don't let any poems stay in the house. Keep them in the mail. A publisher can't buy your poetry if it's on your desk."

FINAL WORDS OF ADVICE

Getting a novel published can be a very long, discouraging process. But if you have a book you really believe in, and you worked hard on it and think it's something good, you shouldn't give up. There is a market out there for first novels, and though it is competitive, it's not impossible to break in. Keep these three tips in mind:

1. Write in the genre you love to read, and be fully aware of the requirements of that genre.

2. Don't be in a rush to send out your material. Polish your work, let it sit for awhile, then go back and polish it again. It's also helpful to get some professional feedback on your work before you submit it. Many organizations offer reasonable critiquing fees (see Appendix A).

3. Familiarize yourself with all the dos and don'ts for approaching editors and agents. A rambling query letter or a sloppy manuscript will quickly turn off the people you want to impress the most.

WRITING NONFICTION BOOKS

"There are no dull subjects. There are only dull writers."
—H. L. Menchken

Nonfiction writers have it somewhat easier than their budding novelist friends. Of the approximately 100,000 books published each year, 85 percent to 90 percent fall under nonfiction. That means that nonfiction writers have many more markets to approach, and their chances of breaking in with that first book are much higher. One step further, a career as a nonfiction book writer is more than possible, and not just for a few lucky lottery-winner types.

NONFICTION CATEGORIES

Here is a list, culled mostly from the current *Writer's Market* (Writer's Digest Books), of all the possible nonfiction categories you could write in.

Agriculture
Alternative Lifestyles
Americana
Animals
Anthropology/Archaeology
Art
Architecture
Astrology
Autobiography
Automotive
Bibliography
Biography
Business/Economics
Child Guidance/Parenting
Children's Nonfiction
Coffee-Table Books
Communications

Community/Public Affairs
Computers/Electronics
Consumer Affairs
Contemporary Culture
Cookbooks
Counseling/Career Guidance/Jobs
Crafts
Creative Nonfiction
Educational/Textbooks
Entertainment/Games
Ethnic
Fashion/Beauty
Feminism
Film/Cinema/Stage
Gardening/Horticulture
Gay/Lesbian
Gift Books

Government/Politics	Picture Books
Health/Medicine	Psychology
History	Real Estate
Hobbies	Recreation
House/Home	Reference
How-To	Regional
Humanities	Religion
Illustrated Books	Scholarly
Juvenile Books	Science/Technology
Labor	Self-Help
Language/Literature	Sex
Law	Social Sciences
Literary Criticism	Sociology
Marine Subjects	Software
Memoirs	Spiritual
Military/War	Sports
Money/Finance	Technical
Multicultural	Translation
Multimedia	Transportation
Music/Dance	Travel
Nature/Environment	True Crime
New Age	Women's Issues/Studies
Philosophy	World Affairs
Photography	Young Adult

Some categories are fairly broad and can overlap the above mentioned topics. For example, "how-to" could cover anything from how to build a deck to how to use a particular computer program. "Self-help" could cover parenting, relationships, overcoming addiction, and so on. When looking for possible publishers remember to look under several different categories your project might fit in.

How you go about marketing your submissions is somewhat easier with nonfiction compared to fiction. While new novelists must have a completed project before approaching an editor or agent, nonfiction writers can have an idea with which they can test the waters, before writing the book. Let's see how that's done.

SELLING, THEN WRITING YOUR NONFICTION BOOK

Often nonfiction writers can sell a book based on a detailed proposal, before they sit down to write the book. If your proposal is well crafted, has all the important information, and convinces the editor you can deliver a professional manuscript, and on time, you might just find a contract coming back in your SASE.

Some editors, however, might be reluctant to offer a contract to a writer with no track record or no real expertise in the subject matter. In this case, you have to decide if it's worth the risk to write the book on "spec" (speculation). If you've done your research, know that there's a place for your project on bookstore shelves, and are a competent writer, it might be worth forging ahead.

What isn't a good idea is to write a nonfiction book first, then start looking for possible publishers for it. Just as with fiction, you have to write to the market—know that there's a niche out there within which your book can fit.

The following six steps to getting your nonfiction book published will show you the ideal procedure to follow.

SIX STEPS TO GETTING PUBLISHED

Step 1: Come Up with an Idea

Sounds simple enough, but make sure your idea is viable and tightly focused.

Step 2: Do Your Research

How many other books are out there covering your subject matter? A simple search on the Internet, at the library, or with Books in Print can answer that question right away. If there are dozens and dozens of books on the subject, it could mean your idea isn't new and original, and it's been done to death.

Don't despair, though. If your book has an original slant, a fresh focus, or a perspective that hasn't been covered, you might be able to keep that project alive. For example, there might be hundreds of books that cover traveling through Europe. But if your book is narrowed down and is, for example, a guide to bike tours on the continent, then perhaps there is room for your title, too. The narrower your focus on a well-published topic, the greater your chances of success.

But don't go too narrow. What if there are very few or even no books on your topic in print? Does that mean you're a shoo-in? Possibly. It could also mean there is no interest in the topic, and publishers won't want to take a chance. Say, for example, your bike tour book mentioned above focuses on only one small city in an area that isn't attractive or accessible to tourists. The audience for this book would be too narrow—and that's why you didn't find other books on the subject.

Researching competing titles is only half of the research you should be doing. You also need to have a good idea as to who would buy your book and how this market would be reached. Are you considering a book on pet care? Then have a rough number of how many pet owners there are in the United States (and Canada, too, possibly) and how many pet shows are held each year where your book might be sold.

Step 3: Target the Markets

After you've done your initial research and see there might be an audience for your book, find publishers you could approach with the project. *The Literary Marketplace* (available in your library), Writer's Digest's *Writer's Market* (available in bookstores or on the Web), and *The International Directory of Little Magazines and Small Presses* (the address for purchasing this book is provided in Appendix B) are the best places to start.

Contact likely candidates and ask for them to send you their catalog. Then you can see exactly what they've already published and where your book may or may not fit. Also ask for their writers guidelines, so if you do decide to approach them, you can offer them exactly what they want. The guidelines will tell you such details as their word count requirements and if they expect authors to provide illustrations.

Step 4: Craft the Query Letter	Just as with writing fiction, your query letter for a nonfiction book must be professionally crafted. The content is different, though. For nonfiction you must include a summary of the book's focus, a rationale for that book (why it should be published), and why you're the one qualified to write the book—all in one page. At the end of your query offer to send a detailed proposal. (See Figure 3.1 for a sample query letter.)
Step 5: Send Out Your Query Letter	Once you have your list of potential publishers, mail your query letter with an SASE to just a few at a time. If you get feedback on your idea, you might discover a need to revise your query. You want to make sure you haven't blitzed all the markets and have no publishers left to query.
Step 6: Craft Your Book Proposal	While you're waiting for those SASEs to come back to your mailbox, get your proposal ready. An excellent guide to help with this is Michael Larsen's *How to Write a Book Proposal* from Writer's Digest Books. In brief, your proposal should include the sections described here.

Proposal Table of Contents. This shows what sections you have included in your proposal and on what page of the proposal each can be found. (It is not the table of contents for your proposed book. See "Sample Table of Contents" following for that.) The following topic headings would be what you include in the proposal table of contents.

Introduction/Overview. This section is your chance to hook the publisher's interest. It should explain your book and make it sound compelling enough that the publisher will want to read the rest of your proposal.

Competition. You want to highlight a gap in the marketplace that your book fills. You don't want to list all the competing titles out there—that won't build a case for your book. Show that there is some competition, but that those books don't cover what you plan to focus on.

The Market. In general, it's the publisher's job to know the market—publishers are already well-aware of school and public libraries, for example. But, if you know about special outlets for selling your proposed book, mention them here.

Format. In this section explain how your book will be laid out, how many parts there are, how many chapters, whether or not illustrations are required. If you're proposing a cookbook, for example, give the publisher an idea of how many recipes will be in each chapter and what kind and how much additional information will be included with each recipe.

Author Bio. Focus your bio on the areas that show you are qualified to write this book. If your proposed book is a history of a particular region, and you happen to hold a Ph.D. in history and are an expert in the field, then highlight that. Proposing a self-help manual for those living "alternative lifestyles"? Make sure you're a qualified professional who has counseled hundreds, if not thousands, of people on these issues.

But what if you're not an expert in any particular field, and it's just your own experiences you have to draw from? Then you've got a tough sell on your hands.

Give your proposal extra credibility by pointing out (both here and in the format section) that you'll be providing quotes and interviews with experts, and consider finding an expert in the field who will coauthor the book with you or provide a foreword.

Sample Table of Contents.   Provide a sample table of contents that names each chapter. You can mention a few of the chapter topics, but no need to go into great detail here. You'll do that in the next step. The sample table of contents is to provide the person considering your proposal with a quick look at what your book will cover.

Chapter Summary.   Give a brief, tightly written paragraph or two, summarizing the focus of each chapter. Avoid a common mistake: don't begin each chapter summary with "Chapter 1 includes, Chapter 2 includes." Jump right into the meat of each chapter.

Delivery.   Some proposals include a section letting the publisher know when you think you can finish and deliver the manuscript. However, this might show ignorance of the publisher's schedule. If you estimate you might need eighteen months and the publisher wants to go to press in a year, your declaration might put you out of the running.

If the book is already completed, then this section would say something to the effect that the manuscript can be delivered upon request. However, it's not a good idea to let the publisher know that the manuscript is finished. The point of the proposal is to get a contract before you actually write the book. What if you've written a 200,000 word tome—and the publisher is interested in only 60,000 words? Certainly, you'll be willing to edit it down—but it's better to wait until you receive a response from your proposal before explaining you might have a monster on your hands. A publisher might be interested in your book and want to work with you producing the finished product. Announcing a *fait accompli* might make the publisher feel pushed out of the loop. The delivery section of your proposal is optional, and often best omitted.

Sample Chapters.   Some proposals include one or two sample chapters, to give the publisher an idea of your book's focus and the style of writing. However, if you're hoping to land a contract based on the proposal, this is a lot of work to do on spec. If you've already written the book, then by all means, include samples. If not, then omit this section and wait to be asked.

Cover Letter and SASE.   If you've sent off a one-page query letter first and received back requests for the detailed proposal you offered, make sure to include a cover letter that performs the following three functions:

• Reminds the publisher that your material is solicited.

• Reminds the publisher in a sentence or two what your proposed book is about.

• Reminds the publisher who you are and what qualifies you to be proposing this book.

Keep the cover letter to less than a page. Make sure you have all your contact information, including your E-mail address. And don't forget to include an SASE for either the return of your proposal or a response.

Writing the Book.   If all has gone well—you did your research, sent out your queries, and followed through with requests for your proposal—you might just find yourself with a contract and a due date. Now it's time to write that book. Don't be afraid of discussing the focus or approach with your editor. But, as with any writing project, it involves applying bottom to seat cushion—sitting there and doing it.

SAMPLE QUERY LETTER

The query letter in Figure 3.1 is one this author and her coauthor used to approach the editors at Writer's Digest Books. Although it took two years and a broadening of the book's focus (it now covers every aspect of getting your novel published, not just the synopsis), Writer's Digest recently published the book with the new title, *Your Novel Proposal: From Creation to Contract.*

DO YOU NEED AN AGENT?

You've just read the six steps to getting published and now you're wondering why contacting agents was not mentioned. While fiction writers usually fare better with an agent representing them, nonfiction writers can often approach publishers alone. There are many more publishers who handle nonfiction than fiction, and often these publishers are open to accepting unagented submissions. In fact, many of the smaller presses rarely are approached by an agent and are not used to working with them. This in part is because most agents prefer to work with the "big guys," where advances and subsequent print runs and sales are usually higher.

If your project is of global interest, you could approach agents first—following the same six steps mentioned earlier. But if your project fits more into a niche market, don't be hesitant to go it alone.

For more information on agents, see Chapter 2.

THE MONEY YOU'LL EARN

As with novels, some contracts for nonfiction books provide an advance against royalties. Others offer a "work-for-hire" or flat fee arrangement. This means that whatever you're paid up front for the book is all you'll see. If the book goes on to be a bestseller, your bank balance will have no cause to celebrate.

Sometimes you have no choice, and, if you think sales might be minimal—it's a small press with small press runs and limited distribution—a flat fee is not a bad idea.

If the publisher is confident, planning a fairly large initial press run of say 10,000 or more, and offers an advance against royalties, you can hope to see some checks down the road once the advance is earned back. (Statements are usually

Figure 3.1 Sample Query Letter

(On your letterhead with your phone number and E-mail address)

Date

Editor's Name, Title
Publishing House
Address

Dear Editor's Name,

One of the nicest moments a beginning novelist gets to experience is typing the words "The End" on the last page of a manuscript. But for many, the sense of accomplishment can often be short-lived. The manuscript is done, but now what? Market-savvy writers know that a polished manuscript is not the only step in making a good impression with prospective editors or agents; how to approach these publishing professionals can carry as much weight as stellar writing. After studying the available literature, a new writer quickly discovers that, along with sample chapters, cover letters, and SASEs, one of the submission requirements is the synopsis. But what's that?

The now frustrated writer will return from the library or bookstore empty-handed. There are no published guidelines on how to write the novel synopsis. Our proposed book, *Synopses*, will fill that huge gap in the marketplace. We cover the different uses of a synopsis, format, the essential elements, mistakes to avoid, and submission strategies.

But, by far, the most exciting component in our book will be the dozens of actual synopses supplied by well-known writers. We have already received contributions from Elmore Leonard, Dick Francis, and Marilyn Campbell and are expecting more. In addition, we have interviewed selected editors and agents for comments on what they look for in a synopsis. These interviews and sample synopses, along with comments from the contributing authors on when, why, and how they wrote them, will guide readers through an often difficult and confusing process and will also enhance the promotability of our book.

Both of us come into contact with several hundred beginning writers each year, through writers workshops and seminars, through the Fiction Writer's Connection membership, through our newsletters, and through referrals. Some of the most frequent questions we receive concern the "dreaded synopsis." Why do we need it? What is it for? What does it look like? How do we write it?

We have designed *Synopses* to answer those questions, and more.

May we send you a full proposal?

Sincerely,

Blythe Camenson and Marshall J. Cook

issued two times a year, and it could be a year or so before sales have earned back the advance.)

Dollar amounts are hard to pinpoint. Some of the small presses offer no advance at all, just a royalty percentage. With this scenario, you have no money coming in while you're writing the book, but at least you won't have to wait to earn back a nonexistent advance. In theory, you should receive your first check with the next royalty period, probably six months from the time your book is on the market.

Other small presses offer advances that range from $500 to $3,000 or so. A large publisher might advance a new writer as high as $10,000 to $25,000, and sometimes more if it's a hot topic and the sales team predicts healthy sales.

AVOIDING FADS

You're back at the Six Steps to Getting Published section, looking at Step 1. You've got an idea and it's hot, hot, hot. You want to stress in your query letter how hot the topic is—and that the publisher should act fast. That's what you *want* to do, but you won't.

Publishers traditionally take up to a year or more for a book to see print. What's hot now will be old news by then. Here's a good example: Throughout 1999 publishers received countless proposals for how to avoid Y2K disasters. On January 1, 2000, all those ideas became obsolete.

Publishers sometimes do put out quickie books—a celebrity or political scandal, for example. O. J. Simpson and the Gulf War come to mind. But, nine times out of ten publishers contact a writer they already know to produce that kind of book.

SELLING THAT SECOND BOOK

If you've followed the six-step program mentioned earlier in this chapter, you've collected a slew of publisher catalogs. Notice how many publishers produce books in a series. Series books cover all sorts of categories: gardening, travel, careers, cooking, and so on. Examine these series carefully to see where the gaps are—gaps that you can fill. A publisher with a sports line, for example, has every book under the sun—except windsurfing. You just happen to know a lot about the subject and would love to produce a book on it.

Studying publisher catalogs works well for coming up with ideas for a first book, but it can also help with future titles, too. Perhaps your first book fit into your publisher's series. You've delivered an outstanding manuscript, you've developed a wonderful rapport with your editor, and now you see ideas for more books to round out their list. At this point, it is perfectly acceptable to make a quick call to your editor to discuss the possibility of additional contracts for you. Your editor might listen to your ideas, then tell you those projects are already under contract. Or you might receive a suggestion to send in a miniproposal and sample table of contents.

Once you have a working relationship established with an editor, that second, third, and even fourth book are much easier to pitch and sell.

And if your first book was a one-hit wonder for that particular publisher, move on. You still have a book to your name, which will add credibility to your proposal to another publisher.

FIRST-HAND ACCOUNT

Martha Hollis
Nonfiction Book Writer

Martha Hollis has a dozen food, travel, and computer technology books to her credit, including the following titles: *The International Breakfast Book* (Macmillan, 1997); *Cooking with the Young and Restless* (Rutledge Hill Press, 1997); *Culinary Secrets of Great Virginia Chefs* (Rutledge Hill Press, 1995); *Palate Pleasures: The Best Restaurants of Hampton Roads* (Dallas: LeFleur Press, 1994); *Whole Grain Goodies* (Dallas: LeFleur Press, 1990); and *High Tech Hits Home* (New York: CBS Computer Books, 1985). She is currently working on a postdoctoral degree in clinical psychology and writing a novel.

How Martha Hollis Got Started

"Initially I was fascinated with computers for home use. I left my job as a professor of decision sciences at the University of San Francisco and wrote the book *High Tech Hits Home*. Deciding I also wanted to write in food and travel, I went to chef school full-time for two years and traveled extensively.

"For my first book, I sent out about twenty proposals to computer-book publishers. I didn't use an agent. It took about four months, but when I got my acceptance in the mail from CBS Computer Books, I was elated.

"The food book genre is tough. The competition is staggering. I self-published five books and marketed them through a whole food market in Dallas while teaching cooking classes. It was a tough way to make money.

"My next published book came about because I was a trained chef. I was invited to be a coauthor with fifty other chefs who were members of the American Culinary Federation [ACF]. Here I received a million-dollar practical culinary education and lots of food. I tested all the recipes with ingredients given by the chefs or paid for by the chefs.

The book is titled *Culinary Secrets of Great Virginia Chefs*. I found the publisher by sending proposal packages, which took over two years, and I handled the contract arrangements myself.

"I finally used an agent for the Macmillan food and travel book. The advance improved dramatically. My next book, *Cooking with the Young and the Restless*, was requested by the same publisher that did the ACF book, Rutledge Hill Press."

What the Work Is Really Like

"Most days I wake up, head straight for my home office, and turn on the computer. While it is firing up I make coffee, handle ablutions, then attack E-mail for my writing warm-up. My "to do" list grows and shrinks, and with a calendar of deadlines it keeps me on track. I write for several hours, then try to take a lunch break and write more after lunch. Every day I reward myself with exercise by hiking, skiing, golfing, or pulling weeds in a 150-foot-square garden.

"As a travel and food writer I need to visit destinations often. I try to schedule a trip at least once a month, usually for five or six days. With a definite project such as *The International Breakfast Book* I would arrange all travel. This book required about three years of travel on a periodic basis and a three-month crunch at the end in Europe and Africa, with a computer and photography equipment in a backpack and minimal clothes in a suitcase. Most of the travel expenses I arrange to have comped by the hospitality client, such as a hotel or airline.

"For projects I am researching on spec—without an assignment—I take press trips arranged by public relations firms, international travel offices, and those needing to promote a particular aspect of travel (tour operators, hotels, luxury resorts, chambers of commerce, food trade associations). This is an excellent way to gather information at a very low cost. I will not take a press trip unless airfare is included. Often it is more expensive for me to stay at home as I have to pay for my own food.

"Back at home it is back to the grind. I download images from the digital camera, catalog slides after processing and organizing notes, then begin to write. For a press trip I like to spin off an immediate magazine or Internet article while saving my favorite parts for my next proposed book.

"When in my technical book phases, I am back to testing software and computer applications. To update the high-tech book, I am working on culinary software, music learning and composing software (with an attached electronic Yamaha keyboard), and home and garden design packages. I am very lucky to have chosen the 'fun' side of computing."

The Upsides

"I love the freedom to choose my major projects. I instigate most of the book proposals on topics that interest me. Research, discovery, and learning are unending and totally fun. (As a professor I also conducted research, but the topics were not that interesting nor pertinent to the lives of real people.)

"Working at home—I am on a mountaintop in a very rural area—is a joy. If I have an answering machine on, I can be totally uninterrupted for long periods. This is crucial for meeting deadlines. Believe it or not, being at home is fun, as I can take a stretch break by vacuuming a room or turning the compost pile or working in one of the gardens. Discipline is crucial to get back to the project. If I am in the proofing stage of a book, I buy a huge jar of jelly candies and reward myself often—proofing is tedious.

"Traveling at minimal expense and dining in the finest restaurants in the world are excellent perks. I also love the adventure-travel experiences (white water rafting, week-long hikes) and meeting people from every walk of life.

"Another upside is the 'amazing factor.' Several years after a book is published, I sometimes read a portion and am amazed that God has given me the gift of writing. Especially in food and travel books, I feel that I am a conduit for people who would not have been otherwise heard.

"During the research phase for the *Breakfast Book*, people wanted to tell me what they had in the morning. They wanted to share their traditions. They were excited that others were interested. They were delighted to be included. It amazed me the responses I received from the finished product. This particular book has helped spread joy in the world."

The Downsides

"The most difficult part is constant rejection by publishers and editors. What I like least is being told that a particular book proposal has no marketing appeal. Sometimes the publishers seem unwilling to break new ground. I have tried self-publishing, but I found both the distribution and promotion difficult. My agent handles my submissions now. I have circulating about twenty proposals a year with about a 5 percent acceptance rate.

"Another difficult part of being a writer is an uneven cash flow. One learns to take on other assignments, such as newspaper work or magazine articles, for short-term cash needs. It is also expensive to buy your own health insurance and pay all the bills.

"Yet another downside is my social life. I miss having lunch with friends on a regular basis. It is difficult at times to stop working and go play with folks. Fortunately, I have to test many recipes. That I do at dinner parties. I also try to select press trips where I know my friends will be."

Earnings

"I have no established salary. In 1985 I received a $4,000 advance. Now my advances average around $30,000 with 10 percent to 15 percent royalties on the net price."

Advice from Martha Hollis

"Take writing courses in college. (I was a business and math major who totally ignored English courses.) Travel every chance you get. Master foreign languages.

"You should possess these qualities: curiosity, tenacity, patience. Be a self-starter and be willing to be a bit different from others. Pay attention to everything around you. Ask tons and tons of questions. Care about those you meet. Be totally honest with your subjects and clients. And maintain your own integrity.

"You also need to have excellent grammar and spelling skills, as well as impeccable organization. A well-rounded background is essential, especially with basic business skills. As an entrepreneur you will probably need to keep your own financial records, conduct your own marketing, and find new outlets for your work.

"Know how to upgrade and repair your own computer or have a friend who is a computer geek.

"People skills are mandatory. Smile frequently. Listen carefully. Be prepared with interviews. Do background research. Check all sources. Ask others for help when you need it.

"To get started, write every chance you get. Letters and E-mails to friends and relatives are excellent practice vehicles. Volunteer to write short pieces for newsletters in your community such as at your church or a local museum. I used to write for an opera guild in Dallas and received tons of exposure from it. I also edited a cookbook for a master gardener group. Bartering was and still is helpful because you can trade your writing skills for something you need or want."

FIRST-HAND ACCOUNT

Jan Goldberg
Nonfiction Book Writer

Jan Goldberg is a full-time writer of both nonfiction books and articles. Her articles have appeared in more than 200 publications, including *Complete Woman, Chicago Parent*, and *Opportunity Magazine*. To date she has more than a dozen books in print, including four Hi-Low career books for children and several VGM Career Books titles (*Careers in Journalism, Opportunities in Horticulture Careers, Careers for Adventurous Types and Other Go-Getters, On the Job: Real People Working in Communications, Great Jobs for Theater Majors*, and more).

Getting Started

"Writing was always my first love. My grandfather was a bookbinder, so as a little girl, my brother, sister, and I would make trips on the weekend to his work place—which was a special treat. I was so enthralled by the excitement of it, with colored pages and scraps of paper and books that seemed to be piled up to the sky—and the smell of it. I can still remember it, and I know it was then that I made up my mind I would do something with books and writing.

"I taught for several years, but still, it was always the writing that interested me. I started with poetry, then did book reviews for awhile. I thought about doing some educational writing and made contacts at Scott Foresman and Addison Wesley and started doing projects for them. I wrote textbooks and activity workbooks, and more and more I decided I preferred writing to teaching.

"Then I contacted an educational publisher that did magazines, and I began to write for *Modern Health* and particularly *Career World*. I started writing career books for NTC/Contemporary Publishing Group and branched out to other publications as well."

The Reality of the Work

"I consider my job to be among the most interesting jobs you could find, especially since I write both books and articles on a variety of subjects. I am constantly researching new subjects and learning something new. I feel as if I am an explorer venturing into new territory every time I approach a new topic.

"I certainly never get bored. Right now, for example, I have two books due next month. I recently rewrote and revised a Camp Fire activity book, and I completed three articles I was assigned. I also attended a writers conference, and I spent a lot of time after that following up with the contacts I'd made with several magazine editors.

"A typical day covers many things: the actual writing, keeping in touch with editors, responding to E-mail, doing research—which might mean going out to the library or using the Internet or phoning in inquiries.

"Everything I do, I do with an eye to the future. What projects will I be working on three months from now, six months from now, even a year from now? I am always planning, always at different stages of projects I am working on."

The Upsides and Downsides

"The good part of all of this is that I can call my own shots and make my own schedule. The bad part is the same, because to meet your obligations and do a good job, you really have to put in a lot of time. Some days could be twelve-hour days, and on other days, depending on deadlines and how many projects I have going on, I might be able to take some time off. Because I work from a home office, I can work whenever I want. But because the work is always there, I never quite get away from it.

"Also, as a freelancer, you're self-employed, basically running your own business. You have to send out bills, keep good records, have several filing systems, and, of course, you have to know how to market and sell yourself well. You're doing anything any small-business person would do.

"What I like the most is the anticipation of new projects, new ideas, being allowed to be creative, and doing new things. But writing is hard work—which a lot of people don't realize—and it isn't always fun.

"For me, the most difficult part is negotiating contracts and trying to collect money that's owed me."

Advice from Jan Goldberg

"You need to have a lot of projects going on at one time if you're going to make a living at writing. As a novice, you have to be patient, otherwise you'll never make it. Getting established is a slow process. You have to pay your dues, as in any other profession. You have to be persistent, and it requires a lot of discipline. You can't really expect too much too soon.

"I've never really figured out an hourly wage for myself, but writing in general is not a high-paying profession. If you want to really make tons of money, you'd probably want to choose another career. Before you think about quitting your day job, you need to be sure how much money you'll be able to make to support yourself."

FINAL WORDS OF ADVICE

These three steps will help you start your career as a nonfiction book writer—and keep it going.

1. Research your book ideas—know the market and find out what gaps you can fill.

2. Learn how to craft compelling and professional query letters and book proposals.

3. Once you're in, develop a good working relationship with your editor.

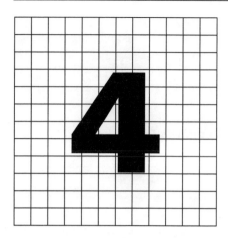

FREELANCE WRITING: MAGAZINES AND NEWSPAPERS

"As an entrepreneur you have to work only half a day—and you get to decide which twelve hours it is."

—Source Unknown

Not all writers write books. Some are happy to work on shorter pieces that appear in a variety of publications, such as magazines, newspapers, and newsletters. (Freelancers who write in other fields such as advertising, public relations, or technical writing are covered in other chapters in this book.)

Freelance magazine and newspaper writers are self-employed and often work from a home office just as novelists and nonfiction book writers do. They generally submit work to more than one publication, although, after getting established, they are often able to develop relationships with different editors that ensure ongoing assignments.

Freelance writers study the various publications—for style and content—then try to meet the needs of those publications by proposing articles on appropriate topics. They spend as much time marketing their work as they do writing it—sometimes more.

DIFFERENT KINDS OF ARTICLES

Articles fall into two broad categories: those that educate and those that entertain. Here is just a small sampling of the topics magazine articles cover:

Art	Food	Pets
Aviation	Gardening	Photography
Business/Finance	General Interest	Politics
Careers	Health	Psychology/Self-Help
Child Care	Hobbies	Retirement
Computers	Humor	Science
Contemporary Culture	Military	Sports
Entertainment	Nature	Travel

(For a more detailed list of topics, see Chapter 3.)

Newspapers are also markets for freelance writers. The following are departments that freelancers often write for:

Business	Fashion
Books	Finance
Entertainment	Food
Health	Lifestyles/Features
Science	Travel
Education	

THE ELEMENTS OF AN ARTICLE

Although the subject matter can be very different, most articles include many of the same elements. They all start with an interesting *hook*, the first paragraph that grabs the reader's (and the editor's) attention. They use quotes from real people or experts, cite important facts, give examples, and sometimes include amusing anecdotes or experiences.

Some articles have *sidebars*, additional information that doesn't fit in the body of the article but is important for readers to know. Examples of sidebars are a salary survey for a career article, "how to get there" information for a travel piece, or a recipe to accompany a cooking article.

The *style* or *tone* of the article will vary according to the publication. Some editors prefer "chatty" pieces that speak directly to the reader; others prefer a more formal voice.

The *content*, of course, would be specific to that particular publication. Travel magazines and newspaper travel sections, for example, print articles on various locales, tips on how to save money when traveling, how to pack, or some other aspect of travel. Certain travel publications use only first-person personal-experience pieces; others prefer third person. Some cover only U.S. destinations; others are markets for exotic travel articles.

By studying a publication and sending for its writers guidelines (a simple request with an SASE will quickly have information in the mail to you), you can see the style, word count, focus, and approach they prefer.

HOW TO GET THAT FIRST ARTICLE PUBLISHED

Study the Publications   Before starting, read as many publications as you can, and in particular, those you would like to write for. Send for sample copies, spend time at the library, or browse through the racks of newsstands. It's never a good idea to send an article to a publication you have never seen before. If you miss the tone or send 2,000 words when they can use only 1,000, you might kill your chances for future acceptance.

What to Write   Some freelancers are generalists and write on a variety of topics—women's issues, parenting, travel, computers—whatever strikes their fancy. They have a wide range of interests and prefer the variety. Others are specialists and focus

their work in one or two particular areas—business and finance or home and garden, for example—and establish a reputation for themselves in those areas.

While specialists limit the number of publications for which they can write,
they often establish relationships with editors more quickly and have an easier
time getting assignments.

Two Approaches

Once you have decided what you want to write about, there are two ways you
can proceed:

1. You can write the entire article on speculation, send it off to appropriate
   editors, and hope they like your topic. On-spec writing is akin to a buck-
   shot approach—fire out a lot of articles and see which ones hit the target.
   It can be time-consuming and not necessarily pay off, but new writers usually have no choice—they have to write on spec before they can establish
   themselves. Editors are often unwilling to give out an assignment to a writer
   without a track record. They want to be sure you can deliver a professional,
   polished manuscript, and on time, before they will hire you.

2. The second approach is first to write a query letter, a miniproposal, to see
   if there is any interest in your idea. Query letters will save you the time of
   writing articles you might have difficulty selling. Only once you're given
   a definite assignment do you then proceed.

DO YOU NEED AN AGENT?

Here freelancers go it alone. Most agents will not handle articles, unless you are
one of their famous clients who also writes books. From reading this chapter you
are now seeing how much work is involved in selling an article. At 15 percent of
$150 to $2,000 or so, the commission check is not big enough to make it worthwhile for an agent to enter this arena.

MARKETING YOUR WORK

Successful freelancers are aggressive marketers. The more query letters or articles you have circulating, the better your chances of landing assignments. Go
through market guides (see Appendix B) and note the possible markets for your
work. Send out query letters on a regular basis—full-time freelancers reveal they
send out forty to fifty query letters a week. That's a lot of work, but no one said
it was easy! However, not all query letters are for brand new article ideas.

Resales

Successful freelancers have learned that writing an article, selling it to a publication, then writing another article to sell to the same or another publication is a
slow way of going about earning a living. They count on being able to sell their
article to more than one publication.

When they come up with an article idea they plan ahead: how many different
markets can this article target?

Unless a publication has bought all rights, and you don't want to sell all the rights to your articles (see later in this chapter for more information on rights), you are free to resell your article as often as you can. However, the rule is that you must approach only noncompeting markets. For example, your travel piece on the "Ten Most Popular Ski Resorts" could appear in the *Washington Post* and the *San Francisco Chronicle*. These two newspapers do not share the same readership. But your piece on "Ten Tips for Keeping Your Cat Healthy" could not appear in both *Cat Fancy* and *Cats Magazine*; they do share the same audience.

Reslant and Resell

Although you can't sell the same article to competing publications, there is a way to resell your pieces to similar markets—with just a little extra work. You've written your piece on "Ten Tips for Keeping Your Cat Healthy" and sent it off to either *Cat Fancy* or *Cats Magazine*. Now it's time to sit back and take a second look at the article. It probably wouldn't take much work to reslant and come up with "Ten Tips for Keeping Your Dog Healthy"—or your horse, or your aquarium, or your pet python.

For every pet there's probably a publication. A quick look at the newsstand or through the market guides will let you know what's out there. A few phone calls to experts in the various fields will give you quotes tailor-made to each article. Or better yet, when talking to that small-pet veterinarian, plan ahead and ask not only about cats, but also throw in a few dog-care questions.

Religious publications are abundant and make very good markets for reslanted articles. *Spiritual Life*, a magazine targeted mostly to a Catholic readership, might use an article on contemporary spirituality. So might the *SCP Journal*, geared toward nonbelievers. While the publications carry similar articles, they have different readership so they're both fair game.

Spoking

Another way to come up with enough article ideas to keep you in business is spoking. Generally, when writers conduct research for an article, they end up collecting more information than they can possibly use in one story. Savvy writers use that extra research to spin off, or "spoke," other article ideas. A successful writer once said, "Give me a city block to write about, and I can support myself for a year; give me a whole city, and I can support myself writing about it for the rest of my life."

The idea of spoking is based on the spokes of a wheel. On page 51 is a diagram of a wheel showing how you can spoke several articles out of the hub's main topic.

Keeping Track of Your Submissions

Accurate recordkeeping is an important aspect of your writing business. You don't want to submit the same article twice to the same editor. Develop a system for yourself that allows you to keep track of possible markets, submission dates, responses, publication dates, and payment and rights information.

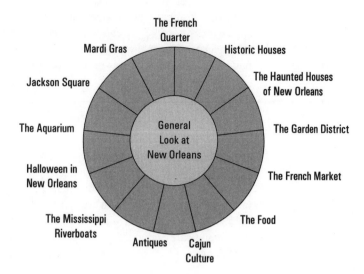

Some writers use index cards (see the interview with poet Linda Addison in Chapter 2), others use computer software specifically designed for this purpose. The more organized you are, the more successful you'll be.

The Elements of a Query Letter

A query letter for an article is similar to one for a nonfiction book. The best queries are one page in length (single-spaced) and start with a hook—perhaps the first paragraph of your article—to grab the editor's attention. The hook is the focus of your piece, the slant that makes it different from all the other articles out there. In the body of your query letter you explain your rationale for the piece and your approach—whether you'll be using expert quotes or not, for example. The bio section of your query letter provides your related credits and explains why you are qualified to write this particular piece. You close by asking simply, "May I have the assignment?"

SAMPLE QUERY LETTER

The query letter in Figure 4.1 proposed an article that was ultimately published in several noncompeting newspaper travel sections. It could also be targeted toward architecture or history magazines.

RIGHTS

When you sell an article to a magazine or newspaper you are offering that publication one of the several types of rights.

First North American Rights

This type of rights means the publication that wants to print your material opts for the right to go to press with your work before anyone else does. Most of the big magazines such as *Modern Bride* or *Women's Own* will prefer to purchase first rights from you. You must wait—sometimes six months to a year—for your article to appear in print before you can sell it elsewhere. If your article never appears in print, and that sometimes happens, you might not be able to sell that piece to another publication, ever, unless you're successful at renegotiating the rights you've sold.

All Rights

All rights means just what you think. The publication is purchasing your article outright, and once you sell it, you no longer own it and are no longer free to make resales. Many of the national magazines such as *Cosmopolitan* prefer to buy all rights. They usually pay enough to make this worthwhile—$1 to $2 a word.

But sometimes, a magazine with a much smaller circulation and a smaller budget for paying freelancers insists on all rights, and then it isn't worthwhile. Freelancers depend on resales to earn their livings. Don't give up right away on a publication wanting all rights, though. Sometimes rights are negotiable. A letter or a phone call back offering first rights or one-time rights might turn out to be acceptable.

One-Time Rights

Ideally, these are the best rights to sell. Most newspapers and many specialty magazines or newsletters request only one-time rights. Again, this means just what it says. They are buying the right to print your article one time.

Second or Reprint Rights

Some publications don't mind if your article has appeared elsewhere. *Reader's Digest*, for example, often uses reprints, as do some smaller publications that reach only a narrow audience.

Electronic Rights

Electronic rights generally means the right to publish your work on the Internet. This is still considered a brand new area—and there has been some controversy surrounding it. Some publishers buying first rights for their print publications have also posted the work on-line—without additional payment to the writers. Make sure you know what rights you are selling, and when in doubt, ask. If the deal doesn't sound like a good one, you can always say no.

THE MONEY YOU'LL EARN

Most writers are thrilled to see their byline, that is, their name in print, giving them credit for the article. And to writers, nothing is more exciting than the finished product, getting to see their stories in print. But even more important to the full-time writer is the paycheck that makes the writing life possible. In the 1700s Samuel Johnson summed it up by saying that no one but a blockhead writes except for money.

It is a well-established fact that writers, for the most part, are underpaid. It's true, specialists in certain fields who have developed an expertise and a good

Figure 4.1 Sample Query Letter

(On your letterhead with your phone number and E-mail address)

Date

Editor's Name, Title
Magazine
Address

Dear Editor's Name,

Most people think of Miami Beach as the place where everyone's grandmother lives. For a long time Collins Avenue and Ocean Drive, packed with residential hotels and condominiums, did cater to the over-sixty set. But in the last fifteen years the demographics, as well as the topography, have been changing.

"Miami Beach is an exciting place to live these days," says Jeff Donnelly, volunteer tour guide for the Miami Design Preservation League. "Young professionals, artists, models, movie production people—they're all flocking here now. We've become very chic."

The old establishments, once painted white and trimmed with only powder blue, aquamarine, or the peaches and pinks of aging flamingos, have now received fresh face-lifts and glow with a contemporary pastel palette. Bands of lavender, blue, yellow, aqua, and a whole spectrum of pinks whimsically decorate oceanfront hotels, sidewalk cafes, model agencies, and apartment buildings. Miami Beach can boast of the largest concentration of Art Deco buildings in the country; over 800 contribute to the historic and architectural nature of the Art Deco District. The result is a Disneyesque urban streetscape, as fanciful as Victorian gingerbread, with the promise of campy humor and fun.

I would like to propose a 1,200-word article, called "Beyond the Beach," covering this exciting section of Miami. Color slides are also available.

I am a freelance writer specializing in travel. My articles and photographs have appeared in over 100 publications including *Newsday*, *Fort Lauderdale Sun-Sentinel*, Gulf Air's inflight, *San Diego Union*, *San Francisco Examiner*, *International Living*, *Accent*, *AAA Going Places*, *British Heritage*, and various others.

May I have the assignment?

Sincerely,

Blythe Camenson

reputation often make more money than generalists. Business and technology publications, for example, tend to pay more than other fields. But still, surveys conducted by the Author's Guild, National Writers Union, and others suggest that only 15 percent of freelancers earn more than $30,000 a year.

Publications usually pay by the word—anywhere from one cent to $1 or $2. This doesn't mean you can earn more money by writing longer articles or padding your piece with extra words. In their guidelines publications state their minimum and maximum word-count requirements, and the editors are certainly professional enough to recognize padding when they see it.

Other publications pay a flat fee—$5 to $1,000 or more for an article, with national magazines at the top of the scale. That's why it's much harder to break into these markets—the competition is fierce, and many of them work only with staff writers. (See Chapter 5.)

Some smaller publications pay only with complimentary copies and a byline. When you query an idea and are given the assignment, discussing payment is usually the next step. Negotiating for more money at this point is not inappropriate. In fact, editors often say they are quite willing to negotiate—and are surprised more writers don't come out and ask for higher fees.

Let's face it. Writers often go into this business not fully understanding that it is a business. Their expertise is with the written word, not with dollar signs and decimal points. But to be a successful freelancer, you have to overcome that mindset, develop a strong business sense, and remember you are selling a valuable product. Yes, there's a lot of competition, with other writers selling equally valuable products. And editors can pick and choose who to work with. But, if you approach the subject with tact and confidence, you won't turn off an editor and send him or her looking elsewhere. Your article is something that editor has decided he or she wants—and might have even given input into its contents—and there is no reason you shouldn't be paid fairly for it.

Having said that, some of the smaller publications just don't have the budget to pay you what your piece is worth. If a byline and a credit is important to you, go ahead with the sale. But be sure to negotiate one-time rights so you can sell the piece elsewhere for additional income.

Some publications will accept photographs or other illustrations with your article—and pay you for each one. Sometimes you'll earn more for your photos than the actual article! One travel writer, who was also an accomplished photographer, realized this early on—and stopped writing articles to focus on creating a stock library of color slides to supply to magazines and newspapers.

As mentioned earlier, resales are the bread and butter for freelance writers. When investigating ideas for articles, keep resale and reslant possibilities in mind. You'll make more money, and in a cost-efficient manner, selling one article to ten different publications, than you will writing ten different pieces and trying to market each of them just once.

It is important to keep in mind that publishers are notoriously slow to pay for your material. Articles are usually paid for in one of two ways: upon acceptance or upon publication. "Upon acceptance" could mean the check will be cut right away—or it could mean four to six weeks later, when the accountant gets around to it. "Upon publication" means that your check will not be issued until the article appears in print. That could be six months to a year from the time you received your acceptance letter. Often your check will be mailed to you with a sample copy of the issue in which your material appears.

With this long lag, you can see how important it is to have as many articles as you can circulating to different publications.

But what if your check just doesn't seem to be in the mail as promised. If repeated phone calls and reminder notes to editors don't work, try contacting the accounting department directly. It is rare for a publication to out-and-out stiff a writer. Sometimes slow payment or nonpayment can just mean a poorly organized staff.

Or it could mean the publication is about to fold or has already gone out of business. If a publication has gone under—either before or after your article has appeared—there is not much you can do about it. Sure, you can pursue legal action, but chances are you are not in the same state as the publication, and the legal fees would end up costing you more than any money you might collect.

Occasionally a publication might purchase your article and promise to run it, then for a variety of reasons, decide not to use it after all. Maybe an on-spec article they like better and on the same topic just arrived, or they changed the focus of the publication, or decided a topic was too controversial, or is now passé. When this happens some publications pay a kill fee—perhaps 15 percent to 25 percent of the agreed upon fee for the article. This should be paid willingly and amicably if they have in their market listings or guidelines that they offer a kill fee. But at least one editor has been quoted as saying, "Yes, we pay kill fees, but then we wouldn't work with that writer again." It's not fair, that's true, but again, there's not much you can do about it. Over time you will learn to pick and choose the editors you submit to and continue to work with. Establishing good relationships with editors is in part how successful writers keep those assignments and checks coming in.

FIRST-HAND ACCOUNT

Joseph Hayes
Freelance Features Writer

Joseph Hayes writes features for a variety of magazines and newspapers. His articles cover people, food, computers and technology, travel, music, and writing about writing. His work has appeared in the following publications: *Fiction Writers Guideline, Gila Queen's Guide to Markets, Inklings/Inkspot, iUniverse.com Nonfiction Industry Newsletter, January Magazine, Jerusalem Report, MaximumPC, Moments Aboard Spirit Airlines, MyMatcher.com, Orlando Magazine, The Orlando Sentinel, Poets & Writers, savvy-HEALTH, Venture Woman,* and *Writer's Journal.* His first article was published in January 1997.

How Joseph Hayes Got Started

"It began as an outgrowth of my 'other' profession: I was a corporate sales trainer for many years, and as such, I developed a skill at taking complicated technical terms and processes and putting them down on paper so they were understandable to ordinary people. My first love will always be fiction writing, but I've been able to take those talents and use them to create what is called creative nonfiction.

"I got started by calling up the local newspaper and speaking to a regional editor. I suggested several concrete story ideas about the community I live in. She liked one, told me to write it, and I've been writing steadily ever since."

The Reality of the Work

"My first duty involves personal accountability—weighing the necessities of getting paying assignments with social responsibility gets high marks. Will I take any assignment, as long as it pays? So far the answer is no.

"Then the duties of the professional writer come in—meeting deadlines, being obligated to deliver the best work you are capable of, regardless of the subject matter, and being in contact with editors once they give you assignments so they know what you're up to.

"I love my job. Not only do I get to (and *have* to) set my own schedule, but I have the opportunity to meet incredible people, people whom I wouldn't ordinarily get to know. The hours are long, and there can sometimes be long gaps between paydays, but I'm getting paid for doing something I've always wanted to do.

"Mostly I write about people, about life. I like to tell stories about ordinary people who do extraordinary things; the guy who sells UFO abduction insurance, the woman who takes photographs of people's auras, the ex–police officer who teaches the bagpipes. My travel articles are about places a tourist wouldn't normally go; my technology pieces are based on helping people understand what on earth modern technology means to them. Bottom line, I'm a storyteller, whether I'm doing it in a piece of fiction or a newspaper.

"Ninety-five percent of my work is generated by ideas I send out. This is called the query process. If it's an editor I know, or have worked with before, I will pick up the phone and give my idea a quick pitch. If it's a new editor or a new publication, I send a letter with a detailed but brief summary of the idea, along with copies of similar articles that I've published before—these are called *clips*.

"In either case, it means that you have to have a very clear and specific idea of what story you want to do. Saying 'I'd really like to do an interview with a band' isn't an idea; it's a daydream. 'I've met the drummer for Back Street Boys and he'll talk to me about the band' is a legitimate article pitch.

"How you decide who to approach depends on what you write. By looking at guidebooks such as the *Writer's Market* and visiting your local newsstands, you get to see what magazines print articles on topics you can write about, which magazines pay, and which ones accept pieces from freelancers.

"A freelancer's life goes through cycles: periods of waiting for work followed by frantic episodes of meeting deadlines. A query can go unanswered for months, but when an editor finally decides he wants the work, he wants it yesterday. This year I had enough time to go on a two-week vacation, and when I got back home, there were six contracts waiting for me, all due in a month!

"I truly believe the job is what you make it. You can be as busy (and successful) as you want to be. Even at this stage, I'm still learning to pace myself when it comes to getting work, and I think I could be doing twice as much writing as I'm doing now if I wanted to, but at the risk of doing lower-quality work than I demand from myself. As it is, I will often put in a twelve-hour day, between writing, researching, and interviewing."

The Upsides and Downsides

"The best part is the freedom, working for myself. Of course, I don't work for myself, I work for magazines and newspapers and editors, but each job has a different boss, and I know if I have a bad experience with one boss, I need not work for him or her again.

"The thrill of stepping up to a magazine rack and seeing your name on the stands is one that I hope will never wear off.

"The bad side is waiting—waiting for an assignment, then waiting for a check. Keeping track of your submissions, your billing, even your expenses, can be tiring and overwhelming, but it's part of the job. A writer only writes part of the time. The rest of the time is spent with details and selling yourself.

"It can also get lonely. Most of the time you are in your office, facing a screen, talking to yourself. And there are times when you have to convince your friends and family that you are actually working even though you are home, and they must respect that."

Earnings

"Someone just starting out can expect to earn very little, if anything. Most freelance writers do it as a part-time thing, and very often they get no pay at all for their work. It's part of establishing yourself in the business and getting experience.

"Once your reputation and skill warrant it, a freelance feature writer can expect to find widely varying pay rates—everything from 5¢ to $1 a word is typical (and some lower than that), while the big, national magazines will pay thousands of dollars an article. But that's a tough group to join."

Advice from Joseph Hayes

"First of all, love language. Love to write. Some writers say they love having written, but hate writing. Such a waste of time! Enjoy every part of the process, sitting in front of the computer or typewriter or notepad, and you'll never suffer from what is called writer's block.

"The article writer should be, first and foremost, an article reader. Be aware of styles of writing, of how things are said. Be a reader, be voracious. Devour facts. Some people keep journals or diaries and jot down observations of people and places. Learn how to put those observations on paper; it's called finding your voice. Writer and teacher Lary Bloom says that voice, the personal voice of the writer, is the most important part of any story; that is, what you yourself add to the article. Remember that only you can tell the story you are telling.

"To start out, find a discussion group at your library or local bookstore, or on-line, and talk about your daily encounters. Learn to listen. Call your local newspaper or church, check the clubs you belong to, ask at local businesses, and see if they have newsletters you can write for. The more words you put in print, the better your words get. And most importantly, never give up! I've been very lucky, being as successful as I've been in such a short time. Some writers take several years of hard work before they see real success. It can be very discouraging, but it's also very rewarding."

FIRST-HAND ACCOUNT

Barbara Stahura
Freelance Writer

Barbara Stahura started her freelance writing business, called Word Worker, in 1994. She writes feature articles, news articles, history books, essays, and newsletters and brochures. As part of her business, she also does proofreading, copy-editing, and editing.

How Barbara Stahura Got Started

"Except for a little poetry (some of which has been published), I stick to non-fiction. I'm basically a self-taught writer. I learned on the job with the utility company I once worked for and have attended various workshops, such as the Iowa Writers' Workshop, the International Women's Writing Guild annual conference at Skidmore College, and Rope Walk in New Harmony, Indiana. This summer I went to Antioch College in Ohio for their workshop. I also read a lot about writing.

"When I was a kid I said I wanted to be a writer but never did anything about it except read everything I could get my hands on. So, when I had the opportunity at around age thirty-six, I applied for a public information writing job with the utility company in Evansville. They hired me, even though I had no previous experience writing on the job (turns out they liked my management experience). I wrote everything, from the company news magazine to speeches to bill inserts. Then, after six years, when I couldn't take corporate life for one more minute, I decided to try my hand at freelancing, figuring I could always get another 'real' job if it didn't work. I was as surprised as anyone that it did work.

"My connections with the utility company helped me find my first clients. And I was also fortunate to connect with several local publishers and editors for whom I still write. I branched out from there.

"My first publication was an essay I wrote, which was originally published in *Science of Mind* magazine, called 'Fearless Self-Employment.' It's all about how I made my decision to leave corporate life, which was killing me emotionally and spiritually, if not physically."

The Realities of the Work

"My duties are to write on various subjects in the style required by the project. Fortunately, most of the things I write about are interesting—or I can work up some interest once I learn about the subject. It helps that I'm a curious person.

"Of course, as a freelancer, I also have to market myself, so I spend time on that every now and then, sending out query letters and so on. I'm not as disciplined about this as I should be, but I get by. Marketing is my least favorite aspect of being a freelancer, but it's probably the most important.

"My job is alternately feast or famine in terms of workload. I'm always trying to even it out, but I doubt if that will ever happen. I work at home, which I thoroughly enjoy because of the independence and freedom it offers. However, since I live alone, it can also be incredibly isolating. I'm often on the phone or E-mailing, which helps, although it's not as satisfying as being with other people in person.

"One thing I like about this job is the variety of subjects I write about. I'm a generalist by nature, so I don't ordinarily specialize. However, over the last year I wrote extensively about Y2K for a variety of publications, including two on-line, as well as *Just in Case*. Some of the other subjects I've covered are high-end fountain pens and jewelry design for a Rolls-Royce publication, microloans, meditation, various artists, archaeological finds, some travel experiences, local and regional entertainment and culture events, and a few computer-related issues. My work has been published locally, regionally, nationally, and internationally.

"I've written several books for a small local publisher: a history of the Indiana Farm Bureau, two county histories, and several histories of military units.

"For two years, I was editor of the Indiana Journal of Commerce and Industry. I began writing for the same publisher on other publications in the early 1990s, when I was still working at the utility. In 1997, when they were looking for an editor, they approached me, and I took them on as another client.

"I'm a senior writer for a Florida publisher, who often contacts me with assignments. I can also suggest my own topics. I also proofread and copyedit for them.

"In the beginning, I did a lot of writing for local businesses, mainly newsletters and brochures. I've dropped most of that since other types of work have picked up. It's actually my least favorite type of writing, but it does pay the bills. (See Chapter 9 for more information on newsletter writing.)

"I'm a radio essayist for the local NPR affiliate. I write and record very short essays that they broadcast during *Morning Edition*. There's no pay, but I enjoy having my essays on the radio. People have told me they enjoyed hearing them, so that's my payoff. I would love to do this on the national level, so I'm getting some of my essays ready to send off.

"It's hard to say if I have a typical day. Some days are mostly research, appointments, and interviews; others I spend mostly writing. Since I can set my own schedule, I can take some time off when necessary—or just if I feel like it. (This is one of the major advantages in being a freelancer, I think.) I make sure that my projects are up-to-date, and if I think an occasional day off would do me some good, I take it. While I might be a little more productive if I had more of a set schedule, having this kind of flexibility fits my personality better. One of the reasons I hated corporate life was having to fit into someone's schedule. Being on my own, I can, for example, go to the gym in the morning and start working later in the day, and then work a little in the evening if I need or want to.

"It's also hard to say how many hours I put in during a week. Anywhere from forty to sixty would be a good guess. When I was just starting this business, I read a great quote that went something like, 'As an entrepreneur you have to work only half a day—and you get to decide which twelve hours it is.' That gave me a good laugh. I don't often work that many hours in a day, although I do when necessary. Since I live alone, it's easy to spend a lot of time working, but I try to keep my life balanced between work and leisure. I'm fairly disciplined—impending starvation is a good motivator—but I try not to be too hard on myself. I take Brenda Ueland's advice in *If You Want to Write*. She says we have to give ourselves time to 'moodle'—which means taking time to relax and play and just not think about much of anything—if we are to be able to recharge ourselves and our creativity."

The Upsides and Downsides

"I most like the freedom to explore and write about subjects I find interesting. The freedom to set my own schedule is also near the top of the list. I like that I get to meet and interview interesting people I otherwise would have no opportunity to talk with. Being a freelancer has broadened my horizons and experience in a way no other job could have done—which is part of the reason I decided to do it. And the longer I do this, the more I learn to trust my intuition about which jobs will be good for me and which will not. I've quit or turned down jobs because they would have been too stressful or boring or didn't fit into whatever plan I had at the moment. I even quit an editing job, even though it was 40 percent of my income, when the management became so dysfunctional that I couldn't deal with them in an honorable way. So far, I've never made a bad decision in that regard. I like that I can test myself in that way.

"The one thing I don't like about this job is having to market myself. It's the hardest and least interesting thing, although the most important. Fortunately, I have many long-term clients who respect my work and whom I enjoy working with. And I've been blessed that new work comes along when I need it."

Earnings

"Before I started freelancing, I read somewhere that the average freelance writer makes $7,000 a year. I knew I could do better than that. And I have. Although my income fluctuates a little from year to year, in 1998 I made more money than I ever did in corporate life—$35,000. My freelance income has always been over $25,000, which is not too bad in this part of the country. As I gain more experience, I keep making more, for which I'm grateful."

Advice from Barbara Stahura

"It's hard for me to give advice to anyone who wants to be a freelance writer. I've never followed the advice in the writing magazines, like have a year's income saved up before you start, or get somewhat established before you quit your day job, although it's certainly worthwhile advice. Because I was so desperate to get out of corporate life, I just jumped off the cliff. Then I worked like a dog and also learned to trust my intuition. I think I'm fortunate in that I did so well right off the bat. Maybe that comes from the contentment I feel with this kind of work. I can't say I've never been worried or scared—because I certainly have—but with my own commitment and the emotional support of family and friends, I've been able to continue and succeed. That kind of support is essential and priceless, so I'd say be sure you have some of that before you begin.

"Another thing that keeps me going is my absolute refusal to ever have a 'real' job again. Maybe that kind of stubbornness will serve someone else well, too.

"However, anyone who wants to try freelance writing needs to be persistent, unafraid of rejection (it's rarely personal anyway), determined, disciplined, patient, and willing to learn. You must be willing to keep improving your skills, and never rest on your past accomplishments.

"Perhaps that's true for any job, but freelancing does not allow you to coast for very long. You must be willing to give up some financial reward, at least in the beginning, and be prepared to live on less for a time. For me, this was something I did willingly, given that my last corporate job that paid well was stressful beyond words. The rewards for me have gone far beyond financial. Being a freelancer has given me the opportunity and freedom to begin finding myself, something that never would have been possible for me in a corporate setting."

FIRST-HAND ACCOUNT

Tanya Lochridge
Freelance Medical/Health Care Writer

Tanya Lochridge writes medical/health care magazine articles, patient education materials, and presentation materials primarily for the consumer/patient audience. In addition, she does some annual reports for managed care organizations and pharmaceutical companies. Her clients include pharmaceutical companies, managed-care organizations, magazines, websites, medical associations, nonprofit associations, and hospitals. She has been freelancing since 1984.

Getting Started

"I knew that writing was always in my soul. I was just not sure a person could actually make a living at it. I grew up in a blue-collar world, and writing was not one of those options that was ever discussed as a career. After teaching for several years, I knew it wasn't for me. I landed a job by coincidence at the only pharmaceutical company at the time in Southern California. I spent about a year working in market research—designing, implementing, and writing various market-research studies. I realized at that point that I could make a living writing.

"While working in market research, I started talking with copywriters and other writers to see what was required for that job and how they reached the position they had. It's strange, all of my work from that point in some way led to my freelance status and success now. I wandered around in the pharmaceutical industry for several years, working in sales, marketing, and education. That experience provides a much broader background than that of most writers—giving me a slight edge."

The Realities of the Work

"Freelance writing has many positives and many negatives. For me the positives far outweigh the negative qualities of the work. Freelancing is not a job for someone who likes the social atmosphere supplied by an office environment.

"My day begins about 10 A.M. or 11 A.M. checking E-mail for assignment updates, and then I write until about three in the afternoon, taking short breaks to stretch. At three I return calls, check with editors or directors on assignments, and then back to writing until about nine in the evening. Although many nights I am up writing until two or three in the morning, depending on the work flow. This schedule is the one I keep when I have plenty of work in the pipeline. If I see assignments slowing—and on a regular basis—I send out a lot of promo materials to existing clients and potential new clients. So basically, if I am not working on a specific assignment, I am working on promotion/marketing. Eighty percent of my time is actually spent researching the topic, and the remaining 20 percent is spent writing.

"Sometimes, to clear my head, I grab the dog and head for the park—what appears to be play to the innocent passerby is really a time for structuring and solving problems in a current assignment."

The Upsides and Downsides

"I like that some days, I can work in my jammies, or a T-shirt and shorts, with my dog keeping me company. I like that I get to use my talents to help consumers and patients at a time when they might be experiencing fear about their health. I like knowing that I can possibly have an effect on someone's life, because the person took the time to read the material I produced, and then took action to seek medical advice. I like that, being a night person, I can work into the wee hours of the morning. I like that I can pick and choose the projects on which I work (although it wasn't always that way).

"What I like least is being the bill collector. Some clients are great and pay invoices promptly, while others make me chase my money. Although, over the years this has become less of a problem since I have weeded out the slow payers by turning down their assignments.

"Sometimes I find it too easy to work around the clock, throwing the balance off in my life. But as a freelancer, you almost have to take all assignments when they come, because there is no guarantee that they will come again next month. So living on a strict budget is a must—no matter how much you earn in a month.

"I don't know how working as a freelancer would work if I had a family to care for—I think that would make it much more difficult. One problem that I had to solve was making friends understand that just because I am home, doesn't mean I'm not busy working."

Earnings

"My annual earnings range between $90,000 and $125,000. However, keep in mind that I have been doing this for years, and I work in a specialty area in which few writers succeed. It takes a certain skill to be able to take 'medicalese' and make it consumer-friendly without talking down to the reader. I believe I could be earning more after all these years, but I am at a point in my life where I am trying to strike a balance between my work and my personal life."

Advice from Tanya Lochridge

"First of all, you've got to be a good writer. So many people today come out of school without writing skills. So be sure that your skills are tops. I believe that part of being a great writer is being an avid reader. Read anything you can get your hands on that fits into the category you are interested in. And read all the stuff you can that just gives you joy.

"Education opens the door, but once you're there you must prove yourself, again and again. It takes a while to establish a reputation in an industry, so be patient, but be persistent. Having the tenacity of a terrier certainly helps in this profession! You also need good researching skills. And don't take rejection or criticism to heart. Use it constructively to improve your skills.

"Develop a promotional package that lists your education, clients, skills, etc. Also include samples of previous work. If you are starting out and don't have previous work, then write some samples that can be included. Don't expect that one promo package will get you the job. Do regular mailings every few weeks (even after all these years, I still mail once a month to all clients and include samples of projects recently completed). I would suggest you work in-house with a company or agency for a period of time—this lends more credibility to your credentials.

"Always continue to learn and upgrade your skills. For example, I started by writing brochures, added newsletters and magazine articles, and now write content for the Web as well. Each of these requires a slightly different set of skills. So, it's best to stay current. Never, ever, miss a deadline—that will be your undoing. Everything you did before will be forgotten and the missed deadline will long be remembered.

"If you want to freelance because you think it is easier than working in an office, think again. As a freelancer, in most cases, you are working in a vacuum, and you do not have the luxury of bouncing ideas off colleagues or just complaining to colleagues about a current project, which can be a relief at times.

"As a freelance writer, you not only complete projects for clients, you also have to complete projects for yourself on a regular basis. There are no paid holidays, paid vacation, paid sick days. Every day you must get up and write."

FIRST-HAND ACCOUNT

Suzanne Casey
Freelance Reporter and Stringer

Suzanne Casey is a freelance reporter and stringer for Central Record Publications, which puts out several local weeklies and monthlies in New Jersey. She also writes feature stories for various publications. She has been writing since 1990.

Getting Started

"I believe it's really a matter of writing choosing me. I have always written. As long as I can remember I kept journals and wrote stories. In the beginning of my business career I started writing for newsletters and business trade journals because I had something to contribute. Getting published was a powerful motivator to keep going.

"I got my first job when I saw a request for articles in a trade publication that I subscribed to. I thought I had to give it a shot and started with a short article on recycling in an office environment. Getting it published motivated me and gave me the courage to try again.

"Years later, when my second daughter was born, I decided to stay at home and combine my freelance writing with a business support service—I am now financially back to the point where I was before becoming home-based.

"I got my current job because a friend of mine was writing feature stories for a monthly publication and gave the editor my name as a possible writer for future assignments. That first assignment has led to a hectic schedule of deadlines for more than four publications under their banner.

"Like a snowball effect, this work has continued to build upon my confidence and allowed me to submit to different (and bigger) publications with a further reach."

What the Work Is Like

"A stringer is basically a part-time or freelance correspondent for a news publication. Some community newspapers or city dailies often don't have enough staff reporters to handle all the stories they need. They use stringers to fill in the gaps. Stringers cover everything from school board meetings to lower interest sporting events to breaking spot news.

"I am fortunate enough to have both a stringer and freelance relationship with my papers. It's a good way to break in for a beginner, too, if you don't mind covering town and school meetings or even sporting events.

"Here's is an example of how I am able to combine being a stringer with freelance writing. I cover zoning and planning meetings as a stringer. I usually report on variances and uses. After hearing month after month about the plans for all the businesses that were coming into town, I turned around and wrote [as a freelancer] a business-page story that covered the explosive commercial growth in a town following its residential boom.

"My duties include research on the Internet and at libraries. I conduct interviews on the phone or in person, and then I write the story. I love what I do—even when the interviewee is tough: either cautious to the point of not talking or doesn't know what to say beyond the one-word response. It becomes a challenge. Overall, I get to meet really wonderful people who do interesting things. I learn about things I would have never known about, so it's always a growing experience for me.

"My articles have ranged from straight news reporting (municipal, school, business) to features (lifestyles, people profiles, arts and entertainment), to advertorials, to theater reviews, to business features. Here and there I also write copy for business material (brochures and marketing pieces).

"While the majority of my stories are assignments, I have some really wonderful editors who support my ideas and welcome my suggestions for stories. It is rare at this point not to have a story idea accepted by one of my editors.

"I had a really wonderful newspaper writer/Pulitzer winner tell me: 'You have to move the furniture around. Everybody has a story to tell; it's up to you as a writer to find it.' Those words have been an inspiration for finding what may not be obvious at first glance.

"The key is to know your editor's needs (or publication's needs). When you're starting out and you hear, 'know your market,' that is really important. Editors respect you more if you're on target and, of course, meet deadlines. (It really makes their job easier, and they appreciate that.)

"So when I run across something interesting I talk to the editor of that section about it. If it doesn't fit, he or she might suggest where it would work better.

"I think I've gotten to the point where I can explore ideas with my editors, and they are open to those ideas. I also keep index cards with subject headings and a list of publications under that. That way if an idea comes up I can check who might be interested in it. Sometimes you can even work the angle of a story in order to fit an editor's needs.

"Because I have young children I will admit some days are harder than others. I work at home and still have a three-year-old with me, who will be going off to preschool two days a week in the fall. My days are somewhat flexible—I can attend school functions during the day when needed or take a walk or bike ride—but it's important to stick to a quasi-schedule of work. Structure and a daily plan are vital to meeting deadlines. If I miss a day because the kids need serious mom time, then I will work later at night to make up the lost time.

"Don't get me wrong, there are days when I enjoy doing nothing but enjoying my family. But small children are the great unknown in the mix. It's really important to have backup baby-sitters, a quiet room to duck into when someone starts wailing unexpectedly, or a mute button on your phone. My kids know that when I'm on the phone, they're not to interrupt me when my hand goes up (except for emergencies). This took some training.

"I usually make all my interview calls first thing in the morning, followed by writing. I try to work on an average of one to two stories a day maximum. This gives me the rest of the day to catch up with people in meetings and callbacks. I have to take a lunch break and a play break for my daughter. Sometimes we hit the library together or work on projects at the kitchen table.

"I sometimes cover meetings at night (anywhere from a half hour to three hours, one to two per week), or events (shows, happenings, etc.). Some events are great for taking the family to or even friends to get feedback.

"At night, after the kids are in bed, I write some more. All my Internet research is done at night as well. My days are never boring, regardless of the work."

The Upsides and Downsides

"I love the work. On 99 percent of my interviews, the people and the things they do are so very interesting. I am constantly learning. And amazingly, one thing always seems to lead to another, whether it is another story idea, or a new contact. Getting the scoop or piece of information that no one else has always feels good.

"The things I like the least are interviewing people who don't want to be interviewed, asking the hard questions, finding out that someone held out some vital piece of information for my story and getting blindsided on it, finding the right angle for the story, and deadlines when things are falling apart around me."

Earnings

"Because I am a freelance writer I am paid by the story. Payments can range from $25 to a couple of hundred dollars in the beginning; better publications pay more. I generally have a lot of things in the mix, so there are various payments for various things—but it all adds up. A newspaper may only pay $25 to $35 per story, but add a sidebar or photos and you can double the amount.

"I have broken $12,000 a year, and I am aiming for breaking $20,000 next year. The catch for me is my children. If I had all day to freely dedicate to my craft, I would be able to increase my income. Because I choose to make my kids my priority, sometimes the writing has to wait.

"I think anyone just starting out as a freelancer should expect to need a cushion for at least a year, maybe more. I think it depends on the time you expect to devote to your writing and, of course, whether a person is any good. I was lucky to have my husband as a strong positive support factor in my career choices. It was a struggle at first, but it has definitely paid off."

Advice from Suzanne Casey

"Keep writing. A good piece of advice I read early on was, 'if you throw enough stuff at the wall, something's bound to stick.' And it's true! Just keep plugging and making contacts. All it takes is one of those contacts to get you published and the rest will fall in line because your confidence and motivation are built up with each one. And with every year you get better and better, and the better assignments come with that."

FINAL WORDS OF ADVICE

Keep in mind three keys to getting your articles published:

1. Make sure your writing is polished and that your articles include all the important elements.

2. Make sure your query letters and manuscripts are neatly typed and free of errors.

3. Make sure you send your articles to the right publication. A magazine that features stories only on "Planning the Perfect Wedding" will not be interested in your piece on "Ten Tips for the Perfect Divorce."

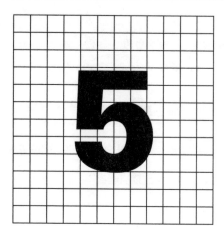

STAFF WRITERS AND REPORTERS

"Writing is the only profession where no one considers you ridiculous if you earn no money."

—Jules Renard

Very few publications are supported solely by freelancers. Most hire full-time staff writers and reporters and depend on these people to fill up the pages with articles or news reports.

Staff writers and reporters don't usually have the luxury of setting their own hours the way freelancers do, and they must come into the office every day. They are given article assignments to research and write, or stories to cover, and they often work with an editor to develop ideas.

While freelance writers have the advantage of being free to come up with their own ideas, staff writers and reporters generally have more job security and always know when their next paycheck will arrive. Freelancers trade job security and regular pay for their independence.

Just as freelancers do, full-time magazine writers and newspaper reporters have to produce high quality work. They have editors to report to and deadlines to meet.

WRITING FOR MAGAZINES

Visit any bookstore or newsstand and you will see hundreds of magazines covering a variety of topics—from sports and cars to fashion and parenting. There are also many you won't see there, the hundreds of trade journals and magazines written for businesses, industries, and professional workers in as many different careers.

These publications all offer information on diverse subjects to their equally diverse readership. They are filled with articles and profiles, interviews and editorials, letters and advice, as well as pages and pages of advertisements. But without writers there would be nothing but advertisements between their covers—and even those are produced by writers!

Working Conditions Writers hold some about 286,000 jobs throughout the United States and Canada. Nearly a third of salaried writers work for magazines and newspapers. Jobs with magazines are concentrated in New York, Chicago, Los Angeles, Boston, Philadelphia, San Francisco, and Washington, D.C.

After receiving an assignment, a staff writer gathers information through personal observation, library research, and interviews. The search for information sometimes requires travel and visits to diverse workplaces, such as factories, offices, laboratories, ballparks, or theaters, but many have to be content with telephone interviews and the library.

Writers then select and organize the material and put it into words, effectively conveying it to the reader, and revise or rewrite sections often, searching for the best organization of the material or the right phrasing.

The workweek usually runs thirty-five to forty hours. Those who prepare morning or weekend publications and broadcasts must work nights and/or weekends. Writers may work overtime to meet deadlines or to cover late-developing stories. They often face pressure to meet deadlines. And with some jobs, deadlines are part of the daily routine.

Job Requirements

A college degree generally is required for a position as a staff writer. Although some employers look for a broad, liberal arts background, most prefer to hire people with degrees in communications, journalism, or English.

It's a good idea while preparing for a career as a staff writer to have academic preparation in another field as well, either to qualify yourself as a writer specializing in that field, or to enter that field if you are unable to get a job in writing.

Writers must be able to express ideas clearly and logically and should love to write. Creativity, curiosity, a broad range of knowledge, self-motivation, and perseverance are also valuable. For some jobs, the ability to concentrate amid confusion and to work under pressure is essential. Familiarity with electronic publishing, graphics, and video production equipment is increasingly needed. On-line magazines require knowledge of computer software used to combine on-line text with graphics, audio, video, and 3-D animation.

High school and college newspapers, literary magazines, and community newspapers and radio and television stations all provide valuable, but sometimes unpaid, practical writing experience. Many magazines offer internships for students. Interns write short pieces, conduct research and interviews, and learn about the publishing business.

Staff writers sometimes start out as editorial assistants and show their talents while on the job, leading them into a promotion. But to get a full-time, permanent position or regular assignments from a publication, writers must be able to show a successful track record and a portfolio of "published clips" showcasing their best work.

In small firms, beginning writers may not only work as editorial or production assistants but also write material right away. They often advance by moving to other firms. In larger firms, jobs usually are more formally structured. Beginners generally do research, fact checking, or copyediting. They take on full-scale writing duties slower than the employees of small companies do. Advancement comes as they are assigned more important articles.

The Competition   According to the *Occupational Outlook Handbook*, through the year 2006, the
                        outlook for most writing jobs is expected to continue to be competitive because
                        so many people are attracted to the field. However, on-line publications and ser-
                        vices, which are relatively new, will continue to grow and require an increased
                        number of writers. Employment of writers is expected to increase faster than the
                        average for all occupations. Employment of salaried writers by periodicals and
                        nonprofit organizations is expected to increase with growing demand for their
                        publications.

                        Many job openings will also occur as experienced workers transfer to other
                        occupations or leave the labor force. Turnover is relatively high in this occupation—
                        many leave because they can't earn enough money.

The Money You'll Earn   According to the 1999 Association of American Publishers, Inc. Survey, com-
                        piled by Buck Consultants, entry-level writers earned a median base salary of
                        $25,500, as compared to $22,600 in 1997. In 1996, beginning salaries for writ-
                        ers averaged $21,000 annually, according to the Dow Jones Newspaper Fund,
                        showing just a slight increase over the past few years.

                        As shown in Chapter 4, salaries for writers are seldom glamorous. But full-
                        time staff writers have the advantage of employment benefits such as health insur-
                        ance, sick leave, and vacation time. Freelancers have to foot the bill for these perks
                        themselves.

WRITING FOR NEWSPAPERS

Do you like being on top of things, always knowing what's going on around you?
If so, a job working for a newspaper might be the right career choice for you.
Reporters, editors, and photojournalists are assigned to a variety of stories, from
the exciting and dangerous to the offbeat and tame.

Those with an adventurous nature might relish the idea of being in the thick
of a downtown riot or chasing fire engines to the scene of a car wreck. Others
might find themselves on the front line in a war zone or witnessing flood rescues
or criminal activity.

For the more sedate, there are specialized fields to cover such as health and
medicine, fashion and food, arts and entertainment.

The departments within newspapers vary from location to location but most
include at least some, if not all, of the following sections:

Art	Fashion
Entertainment	Finance
Business	Food
Books	Foreign Affairs
Consumer Affairs	Health
The Courts	International News
Crime Desk	Lifestyles/Features
Education	Local News

National News	Sports
Religion	State News
Science	Travel
Social Events	Weather

Reporters and correspondents play a key role in our society. They gather information and prepare stories that inform us about local, state, national, and international events; present points of view on current issues; and report on the actions of public officials, corporate executives, special interest groups, and others who exercise power.

In covering a story, they investigate leads and news tips, look at documents, observe on the scene, and interview people. Reporters take notes and may also take photographs or shoot videos. At the office, they organize the material, determine their focus or emphasis, write their stories, and may also edit videos. Many reporters enter information or write stories on portable computers, then submit them to their offices using a telephone modem. In some cases, newswriters write the story from information collected and submitted by the reporter.

General assignment reporters write news stories as assigned, such as an accident, a political rally, the visit of a celebrity, or a company going out of business. Large newspapers and radio and television stations assign reporters to gather news about specific news categories, such as crime or education. Some reporters specialize in fields such as health, politics, foreign affairs, sports, theater, consumer affairs, social events, science, business, and religion.

Investigative reporters cover stories that take many days or weeks of information gathering. News correspondents are stationed in other locations and report on news occurring in large U.S. or foreign cities.

Reporters on small publications cover all aspects of the news: they take photographs, write headlines, lay out pages, edit wire-service copy, and write editorials. They may also solicit advertisements, sell subscriptions, and perform general office work.

Newswriters prepare news items for newspapers or news broadcasts based on information supplied by reporters or wire services. Columnists analyze news and write commentaries based on personal knowledge and experience. Editorial writers write comments to stimulate or mold public opinion in accordance with their publication's viewpoint. Columnists and editorial writers are able to take sides on issues, be subjective, and express their opinions, while other newswriters must be objective and neutral in their coverage.

Working Conditions   Jobs with newspapers are widely dispersed throughout the country. Reporters and correspondents hold about 60,000 jobs throughout the United States and Canada. About seven out of ten work for newspapers, either large-city dailies, suburban and small-town dailies, or weeklies.

The work of reporters and correspondents is usually hectic. They are under great pressure to meet deadlines. Some reporters work in comfortable, private offices; others work in large rooms filled with the sound of keyboards and computer printers, as well as the voices of other reporters.

Working hours vary. Reporters on morning papers often work from late afternoon until midnight. Those on afternoon or evening papers generally work from early morning until early or midafternoon. Reporters may have to change their work hours to meet a deadline or to follow late-breaking developments. Covering wars, political uprisings, fires, floods, and similar events is often dangerous. Their work demands long hours, irregular schedules, and some travel.

Job Requirements

Most employers prefer individuals with a bachelor's degree in journalism, but some hire graduates with other majors. They look for experience on school newspapers or broadcasting stations as well as internships with news organizations. Large city newspapers and stations may also prefer candidates with a degree in a subject-matter specialty—for example, economics, political science, or business. Large newspapers also require a minimum of three to five years experience as a reporter.

Bachelor's degree programs in journalism are available in more than 400 colleges. About three-fourths of the courses in a typical curriculum are in liberal arts; the remainder are in journalism. Journalism courses include introductory mass media, basic reporting and copyediting, history of journalism, and press law and ethics.

Those planning newspaper careers usually specialize in news-editorial journalism. Those planning careers in new media, such as on-line newspapers, require a merging of traditional and new journalism skills. To create a story for multimedia presentation, they need to know how to use computer software to combine on-line story text with graphics, audio and video elements, and even 3-D animation.

Many community and junior colleges offer journalism courses or programs; these credits may be transferable to four-year journalism programs.

A master's degree in journalism is offered by approximately 160 schools; about 30 schools offer a Ph.D. degree. Some graduate programs are intended primarily as preparation for news careers, while others prepare journalism teachers, researchers and theorists, and advertising and public relations workers.

High school courses in English, journalism, and social studies provide a good foundation for college programs. Useful college-level liberal-arts courses include English with an emphasis on writing, sociology, political science, economics, history, and psychology. Courses in computer science, business, and speech are helpful as well. Fluency in a foreign language is necessary in some jobs.

Reporters need good word-processing skills, and computer graphics and desktop publishing skills are also important. A knowledge of news photography is valuable for entry-level positions in combination reporter/camera operator or reporter/photographer.

Work on high school and college newspapers and broadcasting stations, community papers, and Armed Forces publications helps. Experience in a part-time or summer job or an internship with a news organization can also open doors for the new graduate. The Dow Jones Newspaper Fund and newspapers, magazines, and broadcast news organizations offer summer reporting and editing internships. (See Appendix A for more information.) And if you have experience as a "stringer"—a part-time reporter who is paid only for stories printed—that is another plus.

To help finance your education journalism scholarships, fellowships, and assistantships are often awarded to college journalism students by universities, newspapers, foundations, and professional organizations.

Reporters should be dedicated to providing accurate and impartial news. Accuracy is important to serve the public and because untrue or libelous statements can lead to costly lawsuits.

A "nose for news," persistence, initiative, poise, resourcefulness, a good memory, and physical stamina are important, as well as the emotional stability to deal with pressing deadlines, irregular hours, and dangerous assignments. All reporters must be at ease in unfamiliar places and with a variety of people.

Most reporters start at small publications or broadcast stations as general assignment reporters or copyeditors. Large publications and stations hire very few recent graduates; they generally require new reporters to have several years of experience.

Beginning reporters cover court proceedings and civic and club meetings, summarize speeches, and write obituaries. With experience, they report more difficult assignments, cover an assigned "beat," or specialize in a particular field.

Some reporters may advance by moving to larger papers. A few experienced reporters become columnists, correspondents, writers, announcers, or public relations specialists. Others become editors in print journalism or program managers in broadcast journalism, who supervise reporters. Some eventually become broadcasting or publications industry managers.

Getting Ahead

Reporters have to be prepared to move to where the jobs are. You could waste a lot of time waiting for that plum position to open up at your hometown paper. You don't want to have six different jobs in three years, but you should only stay at a paper long enough to utilize everything it has to offer.

And while on the job, be on the lookout for a mentor. Look to someone who is older, more experienced, someone you can trust and who will take your career seriously. A mentor can be invaluable in helping to analyze mistakes so you don't make them again. And if you go to him or her with questions first, you can avoid many mistakes altogether.

The Competition

Competition will continue to be keen for reporting jobs on large metropolitan newspapers. Small-town and suburban newspapers will continue to offer better opportunities for beginners, where the pay is lower.

Many openings arise on small publications as reporters become editors, move on to larger publications, or leave the field. Talented writers who can handle highly specialized scientific or technical subjects have an advantage. Also, stringers and freelancers are being hired by more newspapers. In addition, on-line newspapers should continue to grow very fast and create numerous job opportunities.

Employment of reporters and correspondents is expected to decline through the year 2006—the result of mergers, consolidations and closures of newspapers, decreased circulations, increased expenses, and a decline in advertising profits. Fast growth will occur in new on-line media areas.

Most job openings will arise from the need to replace reporters and correspondents who leave the occupation. Turnover is relatively high in this occupation; some may find the work too stressful and hectic, or they may not like the lifestyle and so transfer to other occupations where their skills are valuable.

Journalism graduates have the background for work in such closely related fields as advertising and public relations, and many take jobs in these fields. Other graduates may accept sales, managerial, and other nonmedia positions, because of the difficulty finding media jobs.

The newspaper industry is sensitive to economic ups and downs. During recessions, few new reporters are hired and some reporters lose their jobs.

The Money You'll Earn   The Newspaper Guild negotiates reporters' wages with newspapers, from starting salaries to the highest earnings, which take effect after three to six years of employment. Variations in salary will occur depending upon the region of the country in which you work. There are certain cities such as New York and Washington that pay high wages, but the cost of living is also much higher.

A beginning reporter at a small paper could start at about $15,000 a year. In a big city, a reporter could start with a salary of $25,000 or so. The average top minimum salary for a reporter with a few years experience is about $34,000 a year.

Salaries for editors usually run higher, but those positions are generally not available to beginners.

FIRST-HAND ACCOUNT

Anne Marie King-Jakubiak
Reporter

Anne Marie King-Jakubiak worked for many years as a journalist with a small-town newspaper in Michigan. She did some investigative reporting and wrote features, movie and theater reviews, and commentaries. She still writes freelance articles and newsletters, but she is concentrating on writing contemporary and historical romances.

She received a Bachelor of Arts in communication with a double major in journalism and English from Madonna University in Livonia, Michigan.

Getting Started   "I was always interested in writing. When I was in grade school I had my first poem published and started winning contests for my writing. I kept a journal all my life on my impressions of people who entered my life and were important. I used to sit at my grandmother's knee and ask for more details of her life as a little girl, when it took twelve hours to ride the horse to town to 'fetch' a doctor. I would beg her for more stories that her mother had told her about the Civil War. Her mother had lived through that era. I have always had an avid interest in what happened, where it happened, and why it happened.

"In high school I took journalism courses and worked on the school paper. I got my first job by walking into a small-town newspaper office and showing them my portfolio of stories I'd done: freelance, high school newspaper, and college newspaper. They needed help; I needed professional experience."

The Realities of the Work

"In truth, being a newspaper reporter was not much fun for me. Editors are always screaming; they don't know how to relax. I've only had one good editor. That was when I was doing investigative reporting. I've heard horror stories about editors picking up typewriters and throwing them at reporters (pre–computer days). The pressure is always on for editors and they take it out on the reporters.

"It was a twenty-four-hour day. Sometimes I would get home only to be called out again. It was not easy, being a single parent.

"When I did a movie or theater critique, I would get two tickets to the play or film. On press night at the plays they would wine and snack us in hopes that our reviews would be favorable. That was fun. Sometimes I'd take a friend or another reporter, or I would take one of my kids. Once, as I was interviewing the guy who use to play Gregg on the Brady Bunch, he stopped the interview to talk to my son who had come with me. Another time I interviewed Sandra Dennis. She didn't care for the town she was playing in. When interviewing, you ask one question, and the response you get usually leads to the next question, if you're good at your job.

"Doing investigative reporting in my case usually led to a front page, five- or six-page series. When I was doing a series on malpractice, I started with the lawyers' point of view. The next story was from the insurance company's point of view, and the next was from the doctors', and then the patient's, and the final story tied it all together. One question led to another, and all kinds of secret documents were sent to me by friends in lawyers' and insurance offices, not to mention doctors I had befriended.

"On another story, I had to interview a security guard who thought he was hot. I quoted him accurately; it's just that when it came out in print he looked like the fool he was. Reporters have words at their disposal that can make or break an interviewee, without once straying from the truth. The words before and after a quote can bring sympathy or make the person look like a fool. An article can be slanted to influence the readers' opinion.

"When I was doing an investigative story about illegal dumping, I got death threats at work and home, if I didn't drop the story. It was a small newspaper and I didn't think anyone really cared. I forgot the Mafia was behind the dumping. My editor didn't. He immediately gave my story to one of the male reporters and pulled me off investigative and onto features. He told me when my last son reached eighteen I could go back. I sort of lost the taste for reporting after a couple of years of features.

"Features can be fun, such as the Valentine story I did on how couples met and what their first date was like. Or they can be intrusive, such as a house fire, or when a child is killed, or when a man has just lost his whole family in an accident. It hurts them to have to answer questions, and I always felt I was intruding on private grief. You have to be sensitive, in my opinion, at those times, and very careful with quotes."

"All in all, the job is more routine than people think. A lot of your work is getting background. You spend time looking into history, law libraries, and public libraries. It's not as exciting as most movies make you think it is. You have to be accurate and quick, and deadlines are always there, and they can't be pushed off for a couple of hours or days. You can't just say, 'oh I can't find that fact, but I'll put it in anyway.' If you don't have background to back you up, don't include it."

"Interviews aren't so bad. You do your homework, you have a small list of points to hit or questions to ask, and then you let it flow naturally. By that I mean that after introducing yourself, and what you're after, you ask the first question giving the interviewee time to answer. If they pause, don't jump in until they finish. That way they may supply more than they should have, because the silence made them nervous.

"I spent a lot of time on the phone to sources and contacts and a lot of time in libraries tracking down background and other information. Contacts and private sources are important—a human voice telling of the experience with all the emotion of human feelings can add a lot to a story. Facial expressions and body language are important. On the phone, the joy or disapproval you hear in a voice can mean a lot."

The Upsides and Downsides

"I loved the excitement—meeting new people and meeting famous people and trying to figure out what makes them tick. "I also loved the digging deep behind the stories and discovering the bad guys.

"I hated the hours and being called out just when I was going to one of my kid's band concerts. I hated canceling plans at the last minute to follow a story or a lead. Also, I still cannot go to a movie or play or read a book without critiquing it."

Advice from Anne Marie King-Jakubiak

"Befriend your contacts; they can become your best sources and also lead to other sources.

"Be careful how you slant a story. I had one editor who didn't want us to check quotes with the sources, giving the source time to rethink and answer in a different way, and another editor who wanted us to recheck.

"You have to love the job and not have as many obligations at home as I did at the time. You have to be naturally curious in order to do a good job and look behind the words and the story. You need a very quick and curious mind. You have to be prepared for anything, and keep your opinions to yourself. Watch your own facial expressions and body language, and be friendly with everyone. You never know who you meet who might in the future become a source, story, or contact.

"You should be able to write well, and keep a fast pace.

"I think taking journalism in high school is important, and keeping a journal as a kid will strengthen your writing skills and curiosity. You should take some college courses if not have a B.A. or even a master's degree. A master's isn't as important, unless you plan on teaching your skill as well. A master's may intimidate your already crabby editor.

"Have a very thick skin. Work well under stress and pressure. Don't plan on a life outside of your job.

"Keep a portfolio of your work. Find a small paper to work at while in college. It will probably be boring at first. Small-town papers like you to start out by reporting on town meetings and other mundane stuff.

"Keep an even temper, and work hard. Be persistent. Get out of the job if you find yourself losing compassion and becoming too cynical. Remember, someone who is in the grips of a tragedy needs to be treated with kid gloves and not be exploited."

FIRST-HAND ACCOUNT

Rod Stafford Hagwood
Fashion Writer/Editor

Rod Stafford Hagwood started freelance writing in college, and in 1990 he moved directly from an internship into his present job as fashion editor at the *Fort Lauderdale Sun-Sentinel.*

Getting Started

"It was not any great career plan. My guidance counselor in high school suggested I consider law, maybe because my father was an attorney, but that really didn't interest me. There were so many rules. I needed to do something where I wasn't strapped in. I was interested in writing, though I didn't really know what to do to make a living out of it.

"I started freelancing for local papers while I was in college, writing entertainment. I got lucky and met a lot of people who helped arrange interviews for me with people I normally wouldn't have been able to reach. For example, I got to interview Tom Cruise right before *Top Gun* came out. And Emilio Estevez and Molly Ringwald. I met George Michael at the premiere of *Pretty in Pink.* We sat down on the stairs, and I interviewed him.

"By the time I graduated, I already had published interviews with all these people, an impressive portfolio, and a job offer with Gannett, which is the parent company of a lot of newspapers, including *USA Today*. They said I could intern at one of their papers and that I'd have a full-time job when I finished.

"I interned at the *Arkansas Gazette*. Again, fate put me in the right place. While getting involved in fund-raisers in Little Rock, I got to meet Mr. and Mrs. Clinton. I wrote about them constantly.

"I got to write about everything. I reviewed classical music, wrote fashion and society pieces. I did everything from flying with the Blue Angels to attending debutante balls in restricted country clubs.

"Even though I already had a firm offer with Gannett, I wasn't sure for what paper I wanted to work. Then the fashion editor of *USA Today* told me about an opening at the paper she used to work for, in Fort Lauderdale, Florida. The job was as fashion editor.

"I knew one person in Fort Lauderdale, and he had a boat. To be honest, I was more interested in getting to spend a weekend in Florida than I was in the interview—I had already been offered a job. I was happy and feeling very secure. Going for the free trip seemed like a fun idea.

"At the interview they wanted to hear my ideas about what I would do as the fashion editor. Because I hadn't taken the job offer very seriously, I hadn't thought of any plans. So I told them the kind of section I would want to write no matter where I was. I wanted it to be very funny, something that was whimsical and didn't take itself seriously. I wanted it to be a little naughty, too—nothing truly offensive, but just so people would say, 'Oh, there he goes again, doing that stuff.' And I wanted the fashion page to have a distinctive voice, that people would know instantly I had written it. They responded well to my answer and made me a very pleasant offer.

"What finally helped me make the decision to take the job was a fashion editor who worked for Reuters. This was about five and a half years ago, and at that time, she said to me, 'That area is it, that's next. Whatever is going to happen in fashion is going to happen in South Florida, in South Beach.'

"I took her advice and here I am. As soon as I arrived, South Beach exploded onto the world stage. And I moved straight from an internship right into an editor's job."

What the Work Is Like

"My main duty is to produce the fashion page, which comes out weekly, on Sundays. Producing means making sure the art is up to the art department's standards, making sure the photography is up to the photography department's standards, and making sure the layout artist gets all the different elements in plenty of time so she can make them fit.

"Then there's the writing, I have to make sure the articles are written, which involves phone calls and research. It doesn't just come tripping off the tongue as people think.

"I cover trends. I'm not going to do a story on Naomi Campbell or Veronica Webb just because they're famous models. But this season, for example, on the runway we saw a lot of Asian models. That's the start of a trend and I'll do a story on that. But I don't cover fads. By the time a fad got in the paper it would be over."

The Upsides

"The ability to define my own rules is an upside. If I'm interested in something, I can go find out about it. It's the only job I know where I can tell my boss I'm heading out to the mall, and that's perfectly acceptable. Last week I went to the beach. I got an item for my column out of it, but the point is I told my editor I'm going to the beach to see what people are wearing when they step off the sand, and she didn't even bat an eye. That's the fun part of the job. If something catches your eye, you can go investigate it.

"Another example is that large, full-service, upscale salons have started producing their own hair products on private labels. I spent four days last week in hair salons being pampered and asking questions like, 'What do you know about chemistry?' or 'What makes you able to produce these products?'

"This is a wonderful kind of freedom, and it keeps you from becoming jaded and tired in your job. You'll never be bored. I can't even think of a downside."

Advice from Rod Stafford Hagwood

"You have to be secure with yourself to be in this business. There are so many extremely insecure and difficult people in the fashion industry. I would have made a wonderful ambassador; you spend a lot of time trying to charm temperamental people.

"I think my parents taught me a wonderful lesson: you have to be the one to define who and what you are; don't let anyone else define you. Being black and a male and a fashion editor, you have to be secure. And if you have that kind of security, you are always in control, and you won't get upset by what other people do."

FINAL WORDS OF ADVICE

Three tips to keep in mind:

1. Before seeking a full-time staff job, try to get some published credits, either by submitting freelance articles to magazines and newspapers or by working as a volunteer or intern on a small paper.

2. Keep a portfolio of your work to show editors.

3. Don't expect to walk right into a plum writing job. Be prepared to start out as an editorial assistant or proofreader.

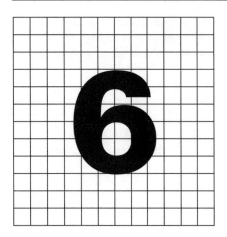

SCREENWRITING

"A screenwriter is a man who is being tortured to confess and has nothing to confess."

—Christopher Isherwood

"Take the money and run."

—Ernest Hemingway

You love going to the movies and you've dreamed about seeing your name roll by on the credits—screenplay by _____ and you fill in the blank.

If you've read Chapter 2, you've discovered how difficult it is to break into the world of print fiction. So you're thinking maybe getting a screenplay produced will be easier. Think again! Although not impossible—thousands of screenplays are made into movies every year, and some by unknowns—the competition is fierce and the process is far more involved than writing and pitching a novel.

While book publishers do spend a pretty penny on each book they publish, the figures are nowhere near what it takes to produce and distribute a movie. If you figure that one top actress earns $20 million per film—that's the current scoop on Julia Roberts—imagine how many other millions must be budgeted to cover the fees of other actors, the camera crew, the director, the producer, the writers, and people responsible for special effects, sound, lighting, location scouting, hair, wardrobe, makeup, travel, food, film, studio time, and so on. With so much money at stake, big-time film producers often prefer to work with big-time screenwriters who have made a name for themselves and have a few Oscars decorating their mantelpieces.

Does this mean you don't have a chance? No, not at all. But, you must know your craft, be dedicated and persistent, know the "tools of the trade," and know how to pitch your work. A little luck wouldn't hurt either.

THE TOOLS OF THE TRADE

Not only must you have a stellar screenplay, as a screenwriter you must also know how to craft query letters, loglines, synopses, treatments, and outlines. Let's look at a definition of each.

Query Letter

Just as novelists, nonfiction book writers, and article writers must have a query letter with which to approach editors and agents, so must screenwriters. The most effective query letter for a screenplay is one page, gives a brief overview of the premise, and provides information about you, the writer. For a sample query letter and an analysis of its important elements, see Figure 6.1.

Logline

A logline is a one- to two-sentence description of your premise. It can be used in person-to-person pitch sessions, in the body of your query letter as an opener to explain your story's premise, or in contests.

Synopsis

A synopsis is a one-page, single-spaced summary of your plot. This differs from the novel synopsis in that it's more of a *selling* tool than a *telling* tool.

Treatment

A treatment can be anywhere from three to fifteen double-spaced pages, describing every scene. Focus on the characters—whose story is this?—and their conflicts, using little or no dialogue.

Outline

Some studios might want to see a step outline, which describes each scene but uses only one line per scene.

SAMPLE QUERY LETTER

Screenwriter Christina Hamlett has provided an example of a query letter for her screenplay, *Everything but the Groom* (see Figure 6.1). Currently three agents have expressed interest. The numbers within the text indicate important elements a query letter for a screenplay should have. An analysis of this letter follows.

Analyzing the Query Letter

(1) Always address your query to a specific individual—and spell his or her name correctly.

(2) It is always beneficial to mention a personal connection, whether to comment on a specific work, to refer to a recent speech or article, or to cite the name of someone who recommended that you initiate contact.

(3) Film companies are always interested in bodies of work that have already been launched in another medium.

(4) Provide a brief overview of what your project is about.

(5) Normally this query letter would contain one more sentence, explaining what Jack's agenda is. Agents and producers don't like teasers, but the author doesn't want to give away the surprise here.

Figure 6.1 Sample Query Letter

(On your letterhead with your phone number and E-mail address)

Date

Producer Name
Studio Name
Address

Dear Producer's Name, (1)

(2) Your name was graciously provided to me by one of your fellow panel members at the recent ASA* Directors Forum. I have followed your work for several years and have recently completed a new script titled *Everything but the Groom*, which I believe meets your studio's standards for contemporary romantic comedy. (3) It is adapted from one of my own novels, which is currently available as an E-book through New Concepts Publishing.

(4) The premise of the story features Kate, a bridal consultant who is contracted to produce the wedding-of-the-century at the private home of a wealthy family in Mill Valley, California. The catch? The too rich/too thin/too snooty bride is marrying Kate's former boyfriend and is taking every opportunity to flaunt her victory and push Kate's buttons. As if matters weren't difficult enough, Kate's regular photographer has an emergency that necessitates him sending an old Army pal, Jack, to cover the nuptials. Jack, however, has his own agenda for being at the Murchie estate that day. (5)

(6) The timeframe of the story covers 48 hours, there are no expensive special effects, and everything necessary for the wedding-day scene can easily be rented from—where else—any place in town that caters to real weddings.

(7) My publishing credits to date include 11 books, 97 plays and musicals, and more than 100 magazine and newspaper articles. I have also worked in radio and cable television, and I am currently teaching an on-line screen writing course through Fiction Writer's Connection (www.fictionwriters.com). (8) Upon request, I would be happy to send you a treatment or the full script, along with a standard industry release.

I look forward to hearing from you at your earliest convenience.

Christina Hamlett

*ASA stands for American Screenwriters Association

(6) Why should a studio take on this particular project? Time, cost, and resources play a big part in what gets picked up and what gets dismissed.

(7) Keep your background information brief, yet demonstrate you've had enough experience for the studio to pay attention to you.

(8) Never send a script unless asked. Many studios won't even open an envelope if it looks as if an unsolicited script might be enclosed.

THE ELEMENTS OF A SCREENPLAY

So far, we've talked about the tools you need to sell your screenplay, but what goes into a screenplay, what makes it salable, and what are producers looking for? Writer Elizabeth English provides some answers in excerpts from her article, "The Making of a Hollywood Film."

THE MAKING OF A HOLLYWOOD FILM

"OK, what is a screenplay? A screenplay is an instrument or blueprint by which words are transformed, by a collaborative effort, into images and sound in film.

"What is the most important part of a screenplay? According to William Goldman, it's the first fifteen minutes, and/or the first fifteen pages. (Screenplays should snap, crackle, and pop on page one! Start with the story in motion, and that scene should foreshadow the story and the ending.) According to actor Paul Newman, though, the most important part of a movie is the last fifteen minutes. The message is clear—give your opening and conclusion equal attention, equal snap, crackle, and pop.

Screenplay Story Components

"1. Most important element? Structure! Act I, II, III. Beginning, middle, end

2. Protagonist, bigger than life, someone with whom the audience can identify

3. Conflict (vital, early on), well-defined

4. Protagonist undergoes some personal or life change by the end of Act I

5. Antagonist(s) should be equal to or greater than protagonist

6. Focus of story—start your story just before or in the middle of the most interesting part

Screenplay Story Structure

"ACT I: Who is the protagonist and what is his/her story? Set up the protagonist's core conflict/dilemma, then introduce other characters. At the end of Act I, give us the most conflict. Now your protagonist should be ready to change toward new direction.

"ACT II: This is where the real story begins, and is the longest part of your screenplay. Robert McKee in his *Story: Substance, Structure, Style, and the*

Principles of Screenwriting tells us: 'A story is built around an active protagonist who struggles against primarily external forces of antagonism to pursue his or her desire, through continuous time, within a consistent and causally connected fictional reality.'

"Screenwriters sometimes have a lot of trouble with Act II. It can seem monotonous, episodic, or aimless. This may be because they've conceived of it as a series of obstacles to the hero's final goal, rather than as a dynamic series of events leading up to and trailing away from the central moment of death and rebirth. At the end of Act II, include the crisis at high point. Some realization of what's at stake has set in for protagonist. There's a confrontation with the antagonist coming up. A moment of truth is about to occur.

"ACT III: This should be no more than fifteen minutes long, resolving all the conflicts. What's the hardest part of the script to write? The ending. The climax usually happens about one to five pages from the end of the script, followed by a short resolution that ties up all loose ends. The big finish, the problem is resolved, the question is answered, the tension lets up, and we know everything will be all right.

"Using a standard Hollywood-required screenplay format will help get the screenplay read. Twelve-point Courier font is a necessity. Two brass brads in white, three-hole-punch paper, ninety to one hundred twenty pages. The title is important, although not always. Producers change titles all the time.

WHAT THE STUDIOS LOOK FOR

"What kinds of movies will the typical big-studio exec greenlight? Formula movies, targeting their main audience: twelve- to twenty-four-year-old males. Then they try to put together hot package deals, with major stars, and/or an A-list director/producer.

WHERE BIG-STUDIO EXECS GET THEIR MATERIAL

- "adaptations of bestsellers

- new versions of old films

- sequels

- copycat films

- TV spin-offs

- comic books

- foreign remakes

"Look carefully at the above list. What you don't see mentioned is original work. The items listed allow for audience recognition and a safer investment. Original work translates to maximum financial risk.

FILM FESTIVALS

"What happens at film festivals? You join crowds of people and mill around, giving each other air-kisses, shaking hands, sipping champagne, reading *Daily Variety*, and talking on your cell phone. There are famous movie stars and directors and producers and distributors. All are being photographed and videotaped, while they smile and schmooze and give interviews to the media.

"And you try to sell your films or screenplays to distributors, buyers, producers, investors, movie stars, directors; you promote and pitch your stuff to people like the Big 5 studios, foreign buyers, Miramax, Fine Line, Dreamworks; you try to find a better agent; you meet foreign filmmakers, you get publicity; you make important contacts; you get financing with the real players, and make deals at film festivals . . . that's all. But none of this comes cheap.

CONTACTS

"Do you happen to know anyone in L.A.? I mean even remotely connected to Hollywood film biz? A friend from school who is the gardener for the shrink of the waiter who serves lunch to the assistant of the guy who sweeps the floors at the office of the personal trainer for Richard Gere's hairdresser's boyfriend? Contacts mean everything.

IS THERE HOPE?

"Here's the Big Question: What makes a film successful? Successful author and screenwriter William Goldman (*Marathon Man*, *Butch Cassidy and the Sundance Kid*) replies, (in an echoing, Godlike voice) the three words that ultimately define Hollywood: 'Nobody . . . knows . . . anything!'"

AN ALTERNATIVE TO THE BIG GUYS

Christina Hamlett, whose first-hand account appears later in this chapter, provides the following information for getting your screenplay in the hands of interested people:

"Aspiring screenwriters today have a number of options available to them in finding producers and pitching scripts. By definition, an 'indie' is a filmmaker who raises his or her own money in order to finance and creatively control a chosen project. Driven by passion more than paycheck, many first-time directors and photographers cut their teeth on independent productions, savoring the heady joy of coloring outside of traditional lines to tell a story their own way.

"In contrast, the studio system assigns all creative decisions to executive producers and/or company heads who, in turn, dictate the style and policies for a hired director. Where studios have the luxury of big budgets, large crews, and Titanic-sized sets, indies function on $10,000 to $500 grand per picture, employ fewer than twenty technicians, and can comfortably fit into premises that would be daunted by gargantuan operations.

"And though many of Hollywood's major stars may decline a role in an indie, just as many are professional enough to take a pay-cut for the chance to push their craft in new directions and, accordingly, widen their options.

"So where does a new writer fit into this equation? The proliferation of indies throughout the country means that writers can find a forum for their work in their own backyard. For starters, every state has a film commission, usually to assist Hollywood productions on location. Such offices also serve as a database of local actors, techies, investors, and writers. Not only does this network benefit indies in search of regional talent and resources, but it also promotes the word that you— the writer—are available to develop and revise scripts. Whether an indie takes you up on that offer depends largely on the existence or absence of a writer-director team, as well as the feasibility of putting your particular story in front of a camera.

"While there are obvious commercial advantages to tailoring projects to an indie's home turf, the only real limits are your imagination and the production's budget.

"As an interesting side note, the book version of my screenplay, *Heaven Only Knows*, is set in San Francisco; the script was adapted to shift the story to the opposite coast. Not only was this beneficial in generating local excitement, but it also eliminated the exterior 'gotchas' of license plates, billboards, foliage, architecture, and weather (just some food for thought if you want to impress a director with your flexibility and sense of economy).

"Four additional routes are available for hooking up with potential directors: trade magazines, screenwriting contests, film festivals, and on-line resources such as indiewire.com. Of these, the last two present the best opportunity for one-on-one interaction, as well as referrals to other filmmakers.

"Cardinal rule: keep your sales pitch succinct. Nothing turns off a director faster than a rambling monologue that begins, 'Something happened to my father's aunt in Dubuque once that everyone says might make a funny movie.'

"The biggest difference between pitching to indies and pitching to studios is that the latter is almost always done by agents. Just as with book publishers, professional reps have the best handle on what their clients are buying and serve as the first level of review in screening the tens of thousands of scripts that cross their desks. The pitch session is essentially an audition that either sends the project on to development or yields the dreaded response, 'Don't call us; we'll call you.'

"Minus the middleman of an agent, an indie isn't governed by such formality, nor are writers left hanging indefinitely as committees debate a script's marketability. Indie writers can expect to play a more active role in the course of a film's development than they would at a studio, where oftentimes 'creative compromise' is penned by someone on staff.

"It also isn't necessary for indie material to have already been audience-tested; i.e., in the form of a published novel or highly acclaimed play. While studios gravitate favorably to established works that represent low risk, indies are in the business of pushing limits and thrusting lesser-known authors into the limelight, forever questing after that rough gem that will ignite into brilliance with just the right polish.

"And although it's helpful to familiarize yourself with a director's past credits to gauge compatibility of your respective visions, it should in no way limit you from pitching your best work, no matter the genre or setting. Probably the worst mistake a writer can make is to assume that whatever genre of storytelling is currently selling will continue to sell. If a script is unique, it actually has a better chance of getting picked up than one that simply imitates ephemeral trends of aliens, talking babies, or Mother-Nature-run-amok. To forget that indies march to their own distinct drummer can mean forfeiting the chance to see your title on a marquee."

DO YOU NEED AN AGENT?

To pitch to the smaller, independent studios, no, you don't need an agent. To hit the big guys, yes. To find agents who handle screenplays, refer to the current *Guide to Literary Agents* (Writer's Digest Books), or the *Literary Marketplace*. If you already have an agent for a book project, check to see if he or she works with subagents for movie rights. Often an unpublished novel manuscript can be shown to film agents and producers and can capture interest—and perhaps a movie option—even if the book hasn't seen print.

Approach a new agent with a query letter (see the sample earlier in this chapter), and close it by offering to send your screenplay.

THE MONEY YOU'LL EARN

If Julia Roberts earns $20 million per film, it's highly likely that the lucky writer or writers working on her screenplays make seven figures, too. Will you? That's highly unlikely. An option on your novel (published or not) could earn you zero, $1,500, or $10,000. If the option is picked up, you could bank another $50,000 or $60,000, more if they actually make your project into a movie.

It's not that the overall money is bad for writing screenplays; it's just so hard to hit the mark that the chances of any money coming your way are pretty slim. Having said that, if you keep at it and never give up, then the odds are in your favor. Don't think in terms of one screenplay—or even twenty. The more prolific you are, the more you study the market and hone your craft, the more you know how to approach agents and producers, the bigger edge you give yourself.

FIRST-HAND ACCOUNT

Christina Hamlett
Screenwriter

Christina Hamlett writes screenplays for Marcia & Company, an independent film studio in Maine. She has four screenplays currently under contract: *Heaven Only Knows*, *St. Scarlett's Ghost*, *Ratt's Race*, and *Rockabye-Bye*.

She has worked in all aspects of media, including cable television, radio scriptwriting, community news reporting, and advertising campaigns. She has also had seven novels and more than 100 magazine and newspaper articles published, and she has written 85 plays and musicals. She does a humor column for several national and regional publications and has worked as an actress and theater director.

She received her B.A. in communications, specializing in audience analysis and message design, from California State University, Sacramento.

Getting Started

"I began writing play scripts in the late 1970s for my touring theater company, The Hamlett Players. It was not only a chance to test material on audiences but also to see what sort of interpretation the actors would apply to their lines and characters. What may sound perfect in your own head while you're writing can come out of a performer's mouth vastly different from what you intended!

"I've always loved a good story, whether it's a book that has kept me reading until three in the morning, or a movie that surprised and delighted me with the quality of its writing and plot twists.

"I'm drawn to film because of my affinity for visuals and dynamic dialogue, not to mention that one day I'm determined to write a part that only Mel Gibson or Tom Selleck can play (and which will require substantive one-on-one coaching by the author).

"The common—and yet intoxicating—denominator of all movies, of course, is that none of them would exist without a screenwriter sitting down to a keyboard somewhere and typing, 'EXTERIOR, TWILIGHT, THE CASTLE . . .'

"My first job out of high school was writing movie and play reviews for a weekly newspaper in Northern California. It not only gave me a byline (and free tickets) and provided a worthwhile overview of both good and bad productions, but it also whet my appetite to see my own name on the big screen.

"I got a newspaper job by convincing the editor that he really needed a movie critic—specifically, me. At that time, the city had two large, competing newspapers, both of which had politely advised that I 'go get a little more experience.' Translation: We're not interested. Stop bothering us.

"My pitch to the weekly was that I could provide a fresh voice on the performing arts. He was either a real visionary or just someone who appreciated I was willing to work for less than minimum wage. That experience then led to a long stint in community theater, the management of my own acting company, and then on to screenwriting.

"Believe it or not, I started working with the independent film company by answering an inquiry posted on the Internet. An ambitious young filmmaker on the Eastern Seaboard wanted to hear from anyone who had written scripts in the genres of comedy or romance. My initial impression was that this person was an acne-faced teenage boy with a camcorder shooting dinosaur-model videos in his parents' garage. I replied to the post just to be encouraging and to offer advice. I was definitely wrong—about the gender, the age, the credentials, and the extent of the dream.

"The filmmaker and I began an E-mail correspondence that led to me pitching the synopsis of an unpublished manuscript that editors at every major house had rejected with the excuse, 'What we're really looking for are books that can be adapted to film.' Less than two months after that first exchange of notes *Heaven Only Knows* was a screenplay in preproduction and yours truly was lead screenwriter for Marcia & Company. (Marcia, by the way, is a dog and our CEO—Canine Executive Officer.)"

The Realities of the Work

"It's a glorious feeling to get paid for doing work you really love. In fact, if it's a perfect fit, it doesn't seem like work at all! Working directly with an indie producer gives me far more feedback and creative control on a project than I think I'd find at a major studio. We do a lot of E-mail brainstorming (I live in California; she's in Maine) and share a common vision of what quality family entertainment should be. If a concept simply doesn't work, neither one of us hesitates to say so. I was also able to bring on board an exceptionally talented composer in New Mexico to write original songs and scores for us. What clicks in this trio of professional dynamics is that, at any given time, two of us are thinking that the third person is really the one with all the talent.

"My primary area of expertise is comedy—regular, workaday people caught up in ludicrous situations made all the worse by their attempts to pretend that they have everything under perfect control. Whenever I'm asked how I come up with my plots and characters, I have to reply that they're derived from years of people-watching and speculating, What if? My own life has been replete with enough odd relatives, neighbors, and coworkers to keep me supplied with funny lines and scenarios for decades. They, of course, never recognize themselves in print nor on screen.

"I'm also fortunate to have a husband who enjoys critiquing my projects and assisting me when I've written myself into mental cul-de-sacs.

"My primary job is to come up with commercial ideas that will work as films. Interestingly, not every book that has ever been written—my own included—would necessarily make a good movie. Every project begins with a rough outline, a lot of give-and-take brainstorming, discussion of potential actors and shooting locales, and then the development of an actual 120-page screenplay.

"In one sense, it's an advantage to have over 2,000 miles between us. If I were on the set every day, I think I would either be (1) too awestruck to function, (2) pestered by actors asking me to explain their 'motivation,' or (3) sent out a lot to get sandwiches and pick up the stars' dry cleaning.

"Although I have an open invitation to visit the set whenever I want, I have the confidence in her talent and judgment to not have to be physically present when those cameras start rolling. In turn, she has the assurance of my flexibility that if a scene isn't working, she'll have a faxed or E-mailed revision in her hands by the time the crew gets back from break. It's the most fun thing I've ever done.

"There's no such thing as a typical or boring day in the film business. When I'm home, I'm usually working on the next script idea or any number of freelance projects, including magazine articles and books. When I'm on a set, I'm absorbed with watching how all the elements come together; I truly don't think

I'll ever grow tired of watching that kind of magic. Plus I rewatch hours and hours of dailies that night and offer input on which scenes work and which don't.

"If there's any level of tedium to the process, it comes from hearing the same line repeated over and over and over. The audience definitely has a misconception of the work actually involved when the final product they see comes off as so seemingly casual and effortless."

The Upsides and Downsides

"Besides the aforementioned joy of seeing a story I've written leap off the printed page and spring to life with real actors, props, and sets, I also subscribe to the philosophy that success is the best revenge. What sweet knowledge it is to picture the reaction of ex-boyfriends, crabby ex-bosses, and snooping former office mates whenever my name scrolls up a screen in capital letters.

"I also view this job as an opportunity to one day segue back into acting by subtly writing into every script a role for a stunning, slender, older woman with quick wit and big hair. What I enjoy least is that there aren't enough hours in the day to write everything that I want!"

Earnings

"Salary with an independent is negotiable and contingent on the total operating budget of the movie. At present, my film income is 5 percent of the total operating budget, plus a percentage of profits. Since the company is only buying the screenplay rights, I retain the freedom to negotiate book, theater, and additional subsidiary rights on my own."

Advice from Christina Hamlett

"Know the craft and the format inside-out before you ever pick up the phone or put a stamp on a query letter to an indie. Just because indies are sometimes viewed as a stepping stone to the big time doesn't mean the quality of work should be that of a novice.

"Write constantly. Go to films of all kinds. Read scripts. Put your best energy into writing the kind of story you yourself would pay those high box-office prices to see.

"Don't go into screenwriting with the objective that you just want to make a lot of money. Maybe you will, maybe you won't. Go into it with the spirit that you want to have fun doing something you really enjoy, and you'll definitely be rewarded.

"Most of all, never forget that the script is the backbone, the essence, the very reason that cameras roll, directors direct, stars are born, and magic unfolds every night on the screens of theaters across the country. Without the writer, audiences would be left sitting in the dark."

FINAL WORDS OF ADVICE

Keep these three tips in mind:

1. Perfect your craft. Read other screenplays, read books on how to write screenplays, and take a screenwriting course.

2. Give your query letter as much attention as you give your screenplay.

3. Don't be afraid to approach independent studios or production companies with your project.

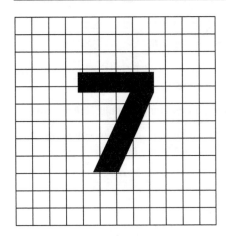

TECHNICAL WRITING

"The difference between the right word and the almost right word is the difference between lightning and the lightning bug."

—Mark Twain

Technical writing is one of our oldest forms of communication. Early technical communicators used cave drawings to convey information about, among other things, how their tools worked and what they were used for.

Modern technology has become much more complex, and it's rare for a single picture to be worth the proverbial thousand words. Today's technical writers are faced with the task of making scientific and technical information easily understandable to a nontechnical audience. They prepare operating and maintenance manuals, catalogs, parts lists, assembly instructions, sales-promotion materials, and project proposals. They also plan and edit technical reports and oversee preparation of illustrations, photographs, diagrams, and charts.

To many, however, "good technical writing" is an oxymoron. Mirroring the Mark Twain quote at the top of this chapter, the difference between good technical writing and not so good can have global impact, as you will see in "Good Technical Writing Should Not Be an Oxymoron," an article contributed by writer and engineer Lisa Eagleson-Roever.

GOOD TECHNICAL WRITING SHOULD NOT BE AN OXYMORON

"Despite the numerous comic strips Scott Adams, creator of Dilbert, has used to poke fun at it, technical writing is not limited to jargon-filled reports translatable only by engineers and nuclear scientists. Technical writing includes any form of business communication not intended to be advertising. Reports, letters, internal memos, guidelines, procedures, training material, and manuals are part of the technical-writing genre.

"Good technical writing, even at its most technical, should not be written to confuse the reader. The letter in Figure 7.1 is a typical business letter, but one that proved to be dangerously ineffective. This letter is part of public record:

Figure 7.1 Technical Writing Sample

Babcock & Wilcox Company

IR Generation Group

TO: [name—Manager, Plant Integration, Three Mile Island]

FROM: [name—Manager, Plan Performance Services, Babcock & Wilcox]

Subject: Operator Interruption of High Pressure Injection (HPI)

References: [two titles listed]

References 1 and 2 recommend a change in Babcock & Wilcox's philosophy for HPI system use during low-pressure transits. Basically they recommend leaving the HPI pumps on, once HPI has been indicated, until it can be determined that the hot leg temperature is more than 50 [degrees] F below Tsat for the reactor cooling system (RCS) pressure. Nuclear Service believes that this mode can cause the RCS (including the pressurizer) to be solid. The pressure reliefs will lift, with a water surge through the discharge piping into the quench tank.

We believe the following incidents should be evaluated:

1) If the pressurizer goes solid with one or more HPI pumps continuing to operate, would there be a pressure spike before the relief valves open that could cause damage to the RCS?

2) What damage would the water surge through the relief valve discharge piping and quench tank cause?

To date, the Nuclear Service has not notified our operating plants to change HPI policy consistent with References 1 and 2 because of the above-stated questions. Yet the references suggest the possibility of uncovering the core if present HPI policy is continued. We request that Integration resolve the issue of how the HPI system should be used. We are available to help as needed.

[signed]

"Did you actually read all that? Probably not. Neither did the plant manager at Three Mile Island.

"That letter was Babcock & Wilcox Company's way of warning Three Mile Island that they could uncover the reactor's core (and thus possibly have a nuclear meltdown) if certain operating procedures were not changed. As you may remember, a nuclear meltdown is exactly what happened.

How to Make Your Writing "Good" Technical Writing

"Use clear, standard language and simple sentences. Define acronyms. Avoid slang (this includes shop talk and terms used inside—but not outside—your work group). When special terms need to be used, define them. Use lists for grouping related items instead of stringing them together in a long paragraph. Use graphs (and use them properly!) to display complex information. Do not use memos and reports as outlets for your creative writing.

"Although Babcock & Wilcox Company (BWC) did define its acronyms, it did not use clear language and simple sentences.

You Have Ten Seconds to Make a Point

"The average reader takes only ten seconds to scan a document and find its purpose before deciding what to do with it. Therefore, the purpose of the document should be up front—either as an opening sentence or on the 'Re:' line.

"BWC failed miserably at being up front. In court, a recipient of the above memo stated that he didn't remember receiving it. Even when it was shown to him and he was told that there was proof he had received it, he still didn't remember ever having read it.

"But, looking at the memo, it's sadly understandable. The point of BWC's memo is in the third-to-last sentence in the last paragraph. The 'Re:' line does not list the key message. If instead it had read 'Possibility of Uncovering Core Exists' the Plant Manager might have paid attention. He understood what could happen if the core were uncovered.

"The lack of time you have to make a point is why you should also think of how your document looks on the page. Sentences should not be much longer than twenty words. Paragraphs should be about six lines. Avoid sentences with all capital letters. Break the habit of writing in passive voice—active-voice sentences sound better to the reader, which makes them easier to read. Use headings to highlight topics. BWC's memo would be easier to scan if it contained headers.

When You Want Action from the Reader

"If you want action from your reader, make certain your purpose contains the phrase 'request for.' Put it at the beginning of your document and again at the end. Often managers and executives skip over the middle of a document and scan only the first and last paragraphs. If they do not see key words like 'request' they will likely put it aside for later. And that means they may never read it again.

"Note that BWC's request is at the bottom of the memo, in the second-to-last sentence. If it had been under a header or on a line by itself, the plant manager at Three Mile Island might have seen it when he scanned the document.

Know Who's Reading Your Documents

"You always think about who your intended reader is, but do you remember to think of the people who will read it after that? With the increasing ease of attaching documents to E-mail, it's likely your report could land on five continents in three days. If your company has offices, manufacturing sites, or distribution centers in other countries, you should assume that your document will leave the United States.

"For this reason the use of standard language in technical writing is important. When in doubt about a phrase, think of how it might be translated by someone with only a common English-to-foreign-language dictionary at his or her disposal.

"And even when your international business partners speak English as a first language or speak fluent English as a second language, read your document carefully before sending it off. American English and British English, for example, use many of the same words for different purposes—some of which are in no way related to each other. Note too that Europeans and Indians who learn English at a young age are more likely to understand Britishisms and Canadianisms than Americanisms."

MAKING A NAME FOR YOURSELF

Will you become famous as a technical writer? It's highly unlikely. In fact, technical writers are often, by necessity, anonymous authors who do not get to see their byline attached to their work. (The exceptions to this rule of anonymity are people who write scientific or technical articles for newspapers, magazines, and learned publications under their own names or write popular how-to guides.)

Why no byline for most technical writers? The next time you try to assemble a child's toy or a new barbecue grill, try to program your VCR or hook up your new fax machine, look on the instruction booklet for the name of the person responsible for the directions—the person you'd like to contact to complain. You won't find it. But that aside, the goal of most employers who produce technical material is to reach their audience with concise and easy to understand language, to promote their product, or to train their audience in its use. No writing stars are required or encouraged.

You can build a name for yourself, though, through your list of credits. Every assignment you land and complete becomes another line to add to your resume. In some cases you might even be able to keep a sample of your work and create a professional portfolio to show to new clients. Word of mouth and employer and client references and recommendations will also help you to become known in your area of specialization.

JOB TITLES

Although the term *technical writer* is the most common job title used, there are other titles as well as ranks:

Assistant Technical Writer

Associate Technical Writer

Consulting Technical Writer

Copyeditor

Copywriter

Corporate Technical Writer

Course Developer

Curriculum Designer

Curriculum Planner

Documentation Contractor

Documentation Specialist

Education Specialist

Information Systems Writer

Instructional Designer

Junior Technical Writer

Knowledge Analyst

Lead Technical Writer

Senior Technical Writer

Software Technical Writer

Technical Communicator

Technical Editor

Technical Intern

Technical Translator

Trainer

TECHNICAL WRITING FIELDS

The number of areas in which a technical writer can work are vast and varied. Most technical writers specialize in just one, sometimes two, areas. A software manual writer wouldn't be expected to be knowledgeable about the environment or advertising, just as a medical writer wouldn't necessarily be familiar with auto mechanics.

The following list of fields is just a guide. Your own research will no doubt help you add to the list.

Advertising

Agricultural

Architecture

Armed Forces

Corporate Communications

Computer System Documentation

Education

Electronics

Engineering

Entertainment

Environment

Film and Documentaries

Finance and Banking

Graphic Design

Government

Information Developer

Instructional Design

Insurance

Investments

Journalism

Manual Writing

Manufacturing

Market Research

Mechanics

Medicine

Multimedia Specialist

Pharmaceuticals

Proposal Writing

Publication Management and Design

Publicity

Public Relations

Research Firms

Sales

Science

Telecommunications

Video Production

Web Page Authoring and Site Design

WHERE TECHNICAL WRITERS WORK

Many technical writers work for computer software firms or manufacturers of air-craft, chemicals, pharmaceuticals, and computers and other electronic equipment. Technical writers are employed throughout the country, but the largest concentrations are in the Northeast, Texas, and California.

TECHNICAL EDITORS

There is a differentiation in most companies between technical writing and technical editing. Editing requires a person who is adept at improving the composition of writing—correcting grammar, punctuation, style, and construction of sentences and paragraphs. Technical writing, on the other hand, encompasses the whole process. It takes in editing, of course, but it extends to original writing as well as the rewriting of other people's manuscripts. The writer must have a firm grasp of the technical material to cope with this kind of assignment.

For the somewhat restricted job of technical editing, it is generally agreed that the person who is trained in English composition will do well. A prospective technical editor should also possess, of course, an affinity for technological subjects and familiarity with engineering and scientific terms. For the writer who must deal in depth with technical subjects, a firm foundation in science and engineering is essential.

For both the technical writer and the technical editor, some knowledge of and aptitude for working with computers and word processors of one kind or another are essential. This includes methods of transmitting information with the aid of computers, information storage and retrieval systems, and various reproduction devices.

JOB OUTLOOK

Opportunities will be good for technical writers because of the more limited number of writers who can handle technical material. Demand for technical writers is expected to increase because of the continuing expansion of scientific and technical information and the continued need to communicate it.

THE TRAINING YOU'LL NEED

Technical writing requires a degree in, or some knowledge about, a specialized field—engineering, business, or one of the sciences, for example. In many cases, people with good writing skills can learn specialized knowledge on the job. Some transfer from jobs as technicians, scientists, or engineers. Others begin as research assistants, editorial assistants, or trainees in a technical information department. They develop technical communication skills and then assume writing duties.

COURSES IN TECHNICAL WRITING

Depending on the university, you will find courses in technical writing offered in many different departments, including the following: English, other humanities-based departments, communications, journalism, business, the sciences, and engineering.

Over the years, colleges and other schools have recognized that engineering students, for example, not only should be taught English composition but also courses in technical writing. These courses are usually taught by members of the English department in an engineering college or by teachers of engineering who have an interest in writing. They deal with special forms of technical writing such as report writing and the preparation of scientific papers and magazine articles.

As a result of the formation of various technical writing societies and the great need for technical writers, industry and the technical presses have taken more interest in what is being taught in colleges. Every year the Institute of Electrical and Electronics Engineers (IEEE), numbering nearly two hundred thousand people, holds a special session titled "Engineering Writing and Speech." During this session, seminars and panel discussions on the training of engineers are held to foster clearer and more informative written communications and to improve the relationships between engineers and technical writers. The result of this two-way process has been the introduction of many fine technical writing courses and four-year programs into a number of colleges and universities.

In addition to technical writing courses, a considerable number of schools now offer majors in this specific discipline. The programs have been given various names and can be found in communication- or humanities-oriented departments under these and similar course titles: science writing, science information, technical journalism, and technical communications.

THE MONEY YOU'LL EARN

The salaries offered to students seeking first jobs in technical writing cannot be definitely established; however, certain basic principles do apply:

- With a bachelor's or master's degree in engineering or science, a student can command a higher beginning salary than a student with a degree in English or some other nontechnical subject.

- Students graduating from certain prestigious colleges usually can command higher salaries than students from lesser-known schools.

- The higher the course grades, the more summer experience obtained, and the more the student can display characteristics of ability and initiative, the higher the salary is likely to be.

- Technical writers with degrees in certain areas, notably electrical engineering and electronics, are in greater demand than students with training in other areas.

- Beginning technical writers are likely to be evaluated very closely on the basis of their educational records, their writing ability, and their potential for being promoted.

According to a recent salary survey conducted by the Society for Technical Communications (STC), the median annual salary for technical writers for the following employment, education, and experience level are as follows:

Entry Level	$36,000
Mid-Level, Nonsupervisory	$42,410
Mid-Level, Supervisory	$47,730
Senior Level, Nonsupervisory	$55,500
Senior Level, Supervisory	$55,900
Bachelor's Degree	$47,300
Master's Degree	$49,460
Doctorate	$59,480
Less than two years	$37,920
Two to five years	$41,650
Six to ten years	$49,810
Eleven years or more	$53,960

The Society for Technical Communication conducts a new salary survey each year. For the most current figures, visit this website: http://www.stc%2dva.org and look under Jobs & Salary Info.

THE JOB HUNT

You should consider employment opportunities long before you graduate from college. In the last few years, a considerable amount of information has been offered about how to get started in technical writing, in the form of ads in newspapers and journals, brochures prepared by the professional societies, professional websites, and even a few books. If you are seriously thinking about becoming a technical writer, you can take a number of steps that will help you obtain professional guidance and information:

- Get in touch with the Education Committee of the Society for Technical Communication. The Committee exists to inform people how to prepare themselves for the profession. It is ready to answer your questions and will send you the names of prominent members of the Society to whom you may write for advice. The STC also maintains a job bank. Their address and website are provided for you in Appendix A.

- The Society for Technical Communication has various publications available on many different aspects of technical writing.

- If you are in high school, make an appointment with your guidance counselor to discuss the profession of technical writing. A lot depends on whether you are planning to continue your education by going to college or taking other specialized training courses. In either case, counselors should have literature available about technical writing careers or can tell you where to find it.

- Don't be shy about talking to professional technical writers or professors of technical writing. This type of information gathering will help make sure you're on the right track with your career choice.

- If you are in college, visit the job placement office. Job placement is a service provided by almost every institution. Throughout the year, college placement offices are in contact with the personnel managers of companies and other organizations that are looking for people to fill important technical-writing jobs.

- Establish job contacts by getting in direct touch with the supervisors and administrators of the publications departments of the companies themselves. To establish these contacts, read the large industrial ads for technical writers in newspapers, especially those in highly developed industrial areas. If you can't find a specific name to send your inquiry to, send it to the director of publications. In time, your letter will filter through to the right person, and you will be able to set up an informational interview—which could possibly lead to a job contact or a full-time job.

- In addition to these methods, don't overlook the ease of finding jobs through the Internet. Websites and databases are updated on a regular basis. The following are websites of agencies and organizations that will help make your job search a bit easier.

    The Computer Merchant Ltd
    Website: www.tcml.com

    DocuClear
    Website: www.docuclear.com

    Documentation Strategies, Inc.
    Website: www.docstrats.com

    Essential Data Corp.
    Website: www.essentialdata.com

    Knowledge Transfer International (KTI)
    Website: www.ktic.com

Northern New England Chapter of the STC
Website: stc.org/region1/nne/www/jobs.htm

Philadelphia Metro Chapter of the STC
Website: stc.org/region2/phi/jobs

PVA Global
Website: www.pvaglobal.com

STC Employment page
Website: stc.org/jobs.html

Targeted Communication Management: Training and Development Job Mart
Website: www.tcm.com/trdev/jobs

Willamette Valley Chapter of the STC
Website: www.teleport.com/~stcwvc/jobs.html

**Sample Job
Advertisements**

To give you an idea of the types of jobs that are advertised, the following samples have been culled from various website databases. Identifying information has been omitted because the jobs will now be filled.

Position: Technical Writer
Location: Connecticut
Job Type: Three-month contract
Salary: Depends on experience
Description: Will be involved in writing a Network Proof of Concept Initiatives. Will write system specifications and will work with core architecture group to write four different specs.
Required Experience: Software documentation experience, Windows NT, SUN, TIBCO

Position: Technical Writer
Job Type: Six-month contract
Location: British Columbia
Description: An intermediate to senior technical writer is required to handle multiple documentation projects (user guides, integration guides, etc.). This Vancouver-based company develops and manufactures touch screens and components, and industrial computers, terminals, and monitors.

Position: Technical Editor
Job Type: Six-month contract
Description: A Montreal firm is seeking an experienced, energetic, and well-organized editor to work in its editorial and production department. Coordinating the tasks of copyediting,

proofing, design, and typesetting of projects from manuscript to printed books or final electronic form. Supervising freelance copyeditors, proofreaders, indexers, and typesetters. Conferring with authors. Being liaison to other departments. Setting and maintaining schedules and budgets. Copyediting and proofreading as needed. Proofhandling, copywriting of cover and promotional materials. Developing capabilities in current technology relevant to electronic editing and publishing.

Required Experience: At least four year's copyediting (preferably on scholarly books); in-house publishing experience; good computer skills (particularly knowledge of electronic editing practices); familiarity with the *Chicago Manual of Style*; management and organizational skills are also an asset.

Salary: Competitive and commensurate with qualifications.

Position: Senior Technical Writer
Job Type: Contract
Location: California
Description: A company is looking for a senior technical writer for a three- to four-month contract to create user documentation for two electronic products for the SOHO market.
Qualifications: The company needs a technical writer with good research and interview skills who can not only create the documentation (write, design, publish) but also create the publishing framework that can be used for future documentation. The company currently works with Word/PageMaker and Corel-Draw but is open to sound recommendations.
Salary: Competitive rates

Position: Senior Technical Communicator
Job Type: Full-time, Staff
Description: In this position you will plan, research, and write installation and administration documentation about MDL server products, database interfaces, and databases. You will develop both hard copy and on-line documentation.
Responsibilities: Plan, research, and write installation and administration documentation about MDL server products and their database interfaces. Work with people in quality assurance, technical support, configuration management, and programming to develop requirements, contents plans, and the technical contents for specific documents. Write documentation based on specifications, other written source information, attendance at meetings, and interview with developers. Update existing documents for new software releases. Plan the contents and quality improvements of specific documents. Participate in the

review and maintenance of product descriptions and functional specifications. Peer review relevant documentation written by other writers.

Qualifications: Bachelor's degree; three-plus years of experience working as a technical writer; experience writing software documentation. Experience writing installation and administration documentation about server products and databases interfaces; familiarity with Oracle databases and their administration; experience with FrameMaker; experience with HTML and Adobe Acrobat; programming experience in C/C++; chemistry background.

Benefits: Medical, Dental, Vision, and 401(k) with matching.

Position: Senior Technical Writer
Job Type: Full-time, On site
Location: Seattle
Description: Senior Technical Writer for a fast-paced, quickly growing, 300-employee, Seattle-based E-commerce company. Work with another Senior Technical Writer to coordinate technical documentation enterprise-wide. Work with Program Managers to identify and write templates for commonly required procedural and technical documents. Work with Program Managers to schedule and edit developer-written design specifications. Work with Documentation team to choose, set up, and maintain a company-wide knowledge base application. Sometimes prepare white papers or visually appealing graphics on E-commerce architectures.

Requirements: English or related degree. Interested in E-commerce. Excellent communications skills with developers and others. Speak geek but write clear English quickly. Should have experience working with developers in helping them produce software design specifications. Should have experience with Internet-based software-development environments. Should know your way around client/server, database-driven Internet application development and know what is involved in documenting it adequately. Should have strategies for dealing with differences between shrink-wrapped versus Internet service-based software environments. Should know the tools of the trade quite well: Word, Visio, RoboHELP or equivalent, HTML-based Help, graphics packages, MS Project. Should have some experience with EDMS. Should know at least one programming language, preferably Java. Should know way around an NT network and ideally should also have UNIX experience.

Position: Manager, Training and Knowledge Management
Job Type: Permanent

Location: New York City

Salary: Approximately $80,000 (depending on relevant experience)

Description: This position exists to ensure accurate, efficient communication of technical, billing, and account information to customers during telephone and electronic interactions. The right person will develop, maintain, and deliver specialized content to care operations personnel; develop and maintain specialized content for customer self-service and internal reference resources; implement a customer-service-skills training program. The main responsibilities of this position are to develop, implement, and maintain training and reference materials for customer operations personnel by researching and documenting appropriate actions and solutions. Also to monitor existing materials and continuously improve them. This position may require 5 percent travel to other company or vendor locations. May require after-hours training delivery.

Experience: Excellent writing skills; strong overall PC skills including MS Project and MS Visio; Word; PowerPoint; knowledge of technical training and documentation tools and methods; experienced with technical writing and Web-based support materials; excellent communication skills.

Contract Versus Full-Time

As you can see from the sample job advertisements, many employers are looking for short-term help, from three to six months. Technical writers who accept these positions are, in essence, freelancers. They contract themselves out to a variety of companies; when one job is finished, they go on to the next. Some people love contracting and wouldn't give it up. It often pays better, although benefits are seldom included, and offers a variety of assignments and experience in different areas.

Other people get into contracting as a foot in the door to a new job market and make the move to permanent employment as quickly as they can. There are also people contracting because their company down-sized and left them unemployed. Some hope to take something permanent as soon as it's offered.

From the employers' standpoint, contracting can be more cost-effective. If they subcontract with other companies to produce specific, time-limited projects, it makes sense for them to budget the fee for a freelancer into their proposal. And with any part-time employment contract, they often can save themselves the cost of health insurance, sick days, pension plans, and other perks offered to full-time help.

Telecommuting

Technical writers who prefer to work at home can find employment where telecommuting is allowed. Telecommuting can mean anything from working almost entirely at home via an ISDN line to your company—you have a direct connection to their network—to being able to take work home with you occasionally. You must, of course, have your own computer with the appropriate applications. If you don't have any meetings scheduled, and you have enough input to proceed, you can work at home, writing without interruption for a day or more.

Engineers (developers) frequently work completely off-site, except for a monthly visit to attend meetings in person. But even these meetings can be attended via teleconferencing.

FIRST-HAND ACCOUNT

Barbara Karst-Sabin
Senior Technical Writer

Barbara Karst-Sabin works on a contract basis for a variety of high-tech companies, focusing mainly on Web-based businesses, writing on-line documentation. She worked for the government for several years, first as a technical writer in telecommunications, then in various other technologies. She also worked as a medical writer. With most of her contracts she is able to telecommute one or two days a week. She has been writing since the late 1970s and earned her master's degree in technical writing and editing in 1986 from San Francisco State University.

Getting Started

"I was always the bright kiddie in the extended family, the one everyone said should become a doctor. My mother, on the other hand, by the time I was six or seven years old, began saying I'd be a science writer. She must have been psychic.

"After a brief career as an artist (I actually was able to support myself), I got a job at a medical school. Because of my background in biochemistry and science in general, I ended up working in the editorial office of the Department of Neurosurgery.

"Much to my chagrin, I could not be hired as a medical writer because I had a bachelor's degree in art, not English. That sent me back to school for a master's. At that time, there was only one degree program in tech/science writing, and that was at Penn State. However, SFSU had a little 'grow-your-own' degree program. To qualify, you had to develop a set of courses that would provide the necessary background—but, they had to come from more than one school, proving that a plain old master's just wouldn't cut it. In addition, you had to have three people in the field review the curriculum you proposed. They had to agree that it would do the trick and that you were capable of not only completing the curriculum, but also of doing the job once you'd gotten your degree. I jumped through all the hoops and—Voila!—had one of the very few master's degrees in tech writing and editing in the world!

"By that time, I'd taken a test for a government job and had been offered a position as a tech writer in telecommunications back East. So that's how I got started, and I haven't done any more medical writing."

Getting a Job

"I worked in Arizona for awhile. Then after I moved back to California I had no contacts in the field and had never really worked in it here, so I started out working on contracts. I found my first one while I was working a contract as a training coordinator in the same company. Now I contact a recruiter I like working with and I post my notice of availability on Dice (www.dice.com) and the head-hunters come to me. I've also gotten jobs through referrals by friends and one at a company where I interviewed for a permanent position before it downsized and dumped most of its writers. When the company was looking for contractors, the manager remembered me because she had wanted to hire me."

The Realities of the Work

"I've written programmer's guides for telecommunications switches, end-user guides for software, troubleshooting manuals for military field communications equipment, recommendations to the Executive Branch on where to spend their science research money in five years, a review of some of the diagnostic tools used in severe head injuries, and developed training courses in the counternar-cotics field and in gourmet and specialty foods. I have also created a website on a company's intranet for their internal documentation, written and produced video news and documentaries, and on and on.

"I love to write and I love learning, especially learning how things work, so I'm the ideal tech writer. I've been assigned to several projects where I was on loan to complete a specified job. However, in most of my jobs, I've been the lead.

"I've also worked several sole writer jobs, which are usually with a group or company that has never had a writer on board and has minimal documentation. In those jobs it's a matter of assessing the problem and determining where best to attack, considering that you are only there for a limited amount of time.

"Most tech writers have to attend regular product and department meetings but spend more of their time in their cubicles. You might spend time in the labs, playing with equipment or software to learn more about it, and you definitely have to spend time working with engineers trying to get the information you need to write your book.

"For me, a permanent job where I would spend all my time writing and updating the same kind of manuals would bore me senseless. I have enjoyed contracting because I know that even a boring job will only last a few months.

"In a big company, with lots of opportunities to move around, you can avoid the trap of sameness, but many people feel comfortable in a routine because it's relatively undemanding. I'm really good at the jobs where they hand you a whip and a chair and throw you in with the lions. It's what I built my reputation on in my government job and the reason I got to do so many different things.

"I'm good at big-picture thinking and at processes, that is, I can usually tell pretty quickly where the process has broken down, and I'm organized enough to know how to fix it. This isn't for everyone, and that's a good thing—more work for me!

"The more usual tech-writing job involves following a style guide and previous documentation to produce a finite number of document types, each of which has certain required types of information to be presented in dictated ways: for example, step-by-step instructions for installing software and reconfiguring your system.

"Most publications managers spend a lot of time in meetings, planning their department's work and allocating resources. Many of them do no writing at all and may not even be writers. At least in the high-tech world, the writer (best-case scenario) is part of the whole product-development process, attending meetings from the time a product is first planned. They will negotiate their deadlines based on the deliverables set by the engineering and marketing members and may work with the engineers during development to begin roughing out their books.

"Many writers act as usability testers since they use the software—installing, configuring, taking screen shots—so they can write their book. They may be the first to see problems or faults and can call them to the developer's attention. They frequently get the product even before the Quality Assurance people do. QA, on the other hand, can help review their documents for accuracy, since they are as deeply involved in the internal workings of the product (hardware or software) as the developers. Because of this working relationship, QA and Tech Publications are often paired under the same management."

The Downsides

"Really bad managers are one of the downsides of this job. The corporate philosophy seems to be that tech writers can't manage, so they put in a former production person who is good with deadlines and getting a book ready to be published, but who tends to be very linear and unaware of some of the compromises that need to be made in formatting to retain the coherence of the material. For example, when giving blocks of code [program], there are certain places you can break a line and have it retain its meaning. If you make the break anywhere else, you've just changed the information. Documents suffer, and you can bet the writer is the one who takes the hit.

"The tech-writing process is frequently a chaotic one. I spent four months at a very high salary trying to prepare a document that never came to be. It took me three months to get the engineers to admit they couldn't make the product work and weren't sure what it would look like or exactly what it would do when it was finished. This didn't stop management from blaming me for wasting their money. At every meeting I reported that there was still no input from engineering, but this was ignored. Too many managers seem to forget that the writer doesn't work in a vacuum. His or her ability to write a document depends on having something to write about."

Earnings

"Salaries are higher here in the Silicon Valley, where I work, than they are anywhere else, including nearby San Francisco. My current hourly wage for a contract is about $60, although I've been offered $65. That's as a senior writer/lead. A junior writer would probably start at $30 to $35. Some writers make up to $80 an hour, but they're usually working independently with no agency fee tacked onto their rate, so they can get more.

"Another rule of thumb is that when you translate contract dollars into permanent salary, you should expect to drop about one third. So, after working at $60 an hour [approximately $125,000 a year], I'm asking $80,000 for an annual salary and finding that acceptable to prospective employers. I should mention that I've been very lucky to have climbed up the salary ladder so quickly. I started January 1998 at $40 an hour and parlayed that into a $60-an-hour contract by January 1999. This is because of my extensive background and isn't a common occurrence.

"Part of the secret, even for a good, experienced writer, is not being afraid to ask for what you're worth. Also, contracting, because of the frequent moves, is probably the best way to move up the 'billable' ladder."

Advice from Barbara Karst-Sabin

"You need to be able to express complex ideas in simple terms. You need to have an interest in technology and to be able to pick up new concepts quickly. You have to be willing to work hard—to learn, to deal with people, to meet deadlines.

"There are a lot of certificate programs available that give the student an exposure to the main kinds of applications commonly used and to the standard document formats—documentation plan, installation guide, user's/administrator's/programmer's guide. This is enough to get you in the door.

"Students in certificate programs can get tech-writing internships to help them get professional experience. Other than that, even those with a great deal of technical background might have to start at the bottom. However, once they have proven themselves as a tech writer, they can quickly move up to an intermediate or even senior position—but they'd probably have to change jobs to do it.

"Join the STC—they have lots of job listings, updated regularly. Last resort is the want ads. The on-line methods are the most cost-effective in terms of the writers' time and energy. When you go that way, a lot of companies will do a screening interview by phone first, saving you a lot of running around. Network if you know other writers or people in the industry you're targeting."

FIRST-HAND ACCOUNT

Jim Cochran
Technical Writer/Producer/Director

Jim Cochran owns his own company, Communications Arts, in Albuquerque, New Mexico. Most of the writing he does is for electronic media, such as video or CD-ROM, with the occasional print article. He deals with a wide variety of scientific, medical, and technical materials. He has been working in the field since 1979.

Getting Started

"I didn't really know I was doing technical writing when I started. The first project I worked with was back in 1978 with the U.S. Department of Agriculture to help explain Title IX, one of their small-farmer grant programs. My next assignments were writing ad copy and developing scripts for marketing and training videos. I liked doing the visual, creative aspects of production and had a talent for understanding complex technical processes, breaking them down into steps, and describing them to defined audiences. This provided me entry into the production world."

The Realities of the Work

"The common thread usually involves learning about a process, then describing it to the defined audience. I use a wide variety of writing styles and presentation techniques within the technical writing genre. I write articles for magazines, copy for marketing materials, both print and electronic, and scripts for CD-ROM and video.

"As an independent producer, I go from project to project. The projects I'm most comfortable with involve developing descriptive presentations. I've developed expertise in nuclear-waste disposal, visual representation of computer processes, and training or orienting people to newly developed programs such as training actuaries on how to explain 401(k) offerings or an overview video for the Defense Department on their new computerized travel system.

"When I first meet with a client to develop a piece of technical communications, I ask some very pointed questions and help focus the client on the answer. I take the time to understand what the client is trying to communicate, to whom, and why. Don't just tell the client you understand what they've told you; communicate it back to them, verbatim if necessary, and get them to understand that you understand. This will establish trust. It's the most important step.

"Come up with a presentation concept that you like, that really turns you on—two, if it occurs to you. Go as big as you can envision—stories, animations, celebrity spokespersons, exotic locations, big props, websites, videos, CD-ROMs—place the idea in a context for them. Then sell it. There is nothing more important nor seductive than vision. It doesn't matter if the idea you started out with requires Mel Gibson as your spokesman in Hawaii, and it ends up with a narrator and shots of the factory floor. The clients will appreciate that they have a visionary working for them. Of course, only experience will give you the ability to know how much the big things cost, but throw them out there. Sell only ideas you're in love with. It will make your work a joy."

The Upsides and Downsides

"I enjoy the information-gathering aspects, the collaborative development of the visual presentation, and the high-profile nature of the end product. One of the great joys of doing technical writing is working with other people who are good at what they do.

"People think technicians and engineers are dry, but I take it as a personal challenge to discover the place in them where their excitement for their expertise lies. There's always a place where a person describing a complex process lights up and begins to talk faster. They are living in their mind's eye and visualizing something complex, yet beautiful in its simplicity. It's what they are visualizing that I want to capture, because that's what will communicate to the audience.

"I dislike it when clients tell me they don't want the presentation to be too flashy, and they underestimate the intelligence of their audience. I don't enjoy it when I can't get the cooperation from content sources, or when the client changes his or her mind about the nature of the content after a crucial step has already been taken. I dislike the inevitable feeling of never knowing enough. And what I really like least about my work is the solitude and focus required to prepare for the parts I like best."

Earnings

"I structure compensation in a number of ways. I try to generate $50 to $75 per hour for my work; however, I may sign on for a project fee and agree on a fixed number of hours up front.

"In a video project, I may charge $100 to $450 per finished minute of script. This refers to the number of minutes the finished video will be. This charge includes all of the research and rewrites. I have an advantage in writing video scripts because I know what will be expensive to shoot and what won't.

"Starting out, you should take what you can get. Experience and learning are everything; money is nothing. Eat salad."

Advice from Jim Cochran

"Don't fake it! The only way you become competent and therefore valuable is to start out incompetent. Don't pretend to know what you don't, but don't be afraid to take on challenges and work extra hours. Make up for inexperience with enthusiasm. Seek out people who are better than you, no matter how good you get.

"I think that there is a myth that technical writing does not require creativity. Not true. All good communication requires creativity. I believe placing the content within the context of a story is essential to comprehension and retention. In order to put your point across, you need to establish a context or a framework in which the information is functional.

"Telling the story of a single tree as it crashes to the forest floor, moves through the woods to a truck, its journey over rough roads to the sawmill to a scene of a table being delivered to a house in your neighborhood is more compelling and memorable than a step-by-step process analysis.

"The only real joy in work is doing something you love and getting good at it. If I were just starting out, I would look for work in the marketing department of a small company, ad agency, or PR firm. You will get a wide range of experience in various media and be required to generate copy for everything from brochures to ad copy to instruction manuals."

FIRST-HAND ACCOUNT

Kathleen Frost
Documentation Specialist

Kathleen Frost works for Magnet Communications, Inc., an Internet banking software company in Atlanta, Georgia. She has been in the field since 1985 and has learned much of what she knows on the job. She also participated in a proposal writing and technical editing program at Southern Tech in Atlanta.

Getting Started

"I needed to support myself and had written four published articles. I also tried my hand at fiction. I was shocked to learn that I could write and get paid for doing something that came easily to me.

"With my first technical-writing job, a company was willing to take a chance on me based on my writing ability. They trained me in their method of writing self-paced training materials and sent me to work in a nuclear power plant in Homestead, Florida.

"I got my current position because I had enough variety in contracts over the past seven years to fit all their needs as the only documentation person in a small, fast-growing company. My background also proved I was capable of taking on the management position when the company was ready to hire more people in the documentation department."

The Realities of the Work

"I specialize in computer and software documentation and training. I always think of technical writing as translating the computerese practiced by programmers and technical people to the everyday English needed by a customer to use the product. No matter what media I am using, the job involves training users.

"You have to be able to identify with the product users because they are looking at the product from the application side of the equation, not the planning and programming side that your in-house developers see. More and more companies are realizing how important good documentation is to a salable, profitable product.

"You have to be the user representative, helping to plan the user interface, making sure labels, screen, and button actions are consistent, so the user won't get lost. You also plan the product library to give users the information they need in an easy to use format.

"Sometimes, you have to be firm with developers to be sure they understand that the product is being developed for the user, not for their exercise in fancy programming. In the end, the users only see a screen and the manual or on-line help to tell them how to use it. Their impression of the application is only as good as these two pieces. They are not interested in the length or cost or number of lines of code written. If the product doesn't work as advertised, they are frustrated and sometimes angry. The company loses its word of mouth advertising and repeat sales.

"In my present company, we work with high-profile banks who buy our products and sell the associated services to their big corporate clients. In our contracts we state that the product comes with on-line help and documentation. More and more of our customers are asking up front during preliminary negotiations to see samples of the documentation that will go to them and to the end users. Many also want to know how to customize the help and documents with their logo and preferred colors, before they even buy the product.

"Documentation is a big selling point for us. I write on-line help for both the bank and end-user services, large product manuals that describe all the services with that product and how to set them up, and manuals on concepts that cover multiple products. I also do technical documents for installation and support, programming reference manuals, and some marketing overview material. The training department is hiring a trainer who will work 50 percent of the time with me to write the training materials under my direction.

"I have been writing in this industry long enough to know what types of documents are typical for a software release. I also suggest new documents—either adding or revising help or writing a quick reference or full manual—on subjects that customers ask about frequently.

"Depending on how quickly the next release is sneaking up on me, my day can be busy or relaxed. I am often answering requests, either directly from a customer or one passed on from the customer relations manager or a customer service representative.

"Other times, I work on a manual, interviewing the programmers or product managers to determine how the product works and what to tell the user.

"I thought the original help system was ugly, boring, and had too much background information for the user to find the instructions easily. I designed a completely new on-line help system, did a prototype, got it approved, and started converting all the existing help to the new program. Management was impressed enough to schedule a separate release of the help system to promote what we've done."

The Upsides and Downsides

"I find the work interesting because there is always something new to do. We have a very fast-paced office. I am in the middle of verifying and editing all the documentation done before I arrived, as well as writing help and overviews for all the new services as they are developed.

"I get to work with the application in the test environment, suggest user-related changes in the interface, and point out whether labels and actions are consistent. I even get involved in final testing and QA.

"This is a strong team environment, so I participate in everything from initial planning to the final testing and release notes. This particular company is growing fast and should go public sometime next year. I am fortunate to have stock options and 50 percent telecommuting. Other jobs with more established companies would be more specialized. You might be responsible for just one or two manuals for each release or just on-line help, designing reports or a production/graphics position. Because I am the only writer at the moment, I have to do it all.

"What I like least are jobs where I have a set product, only one product, and have to do revisions for the same manual over and over for consecutive releases. This kind of job can be so boring, you look for a new position to do something different."

Advice from Kathleen Frost

"Many colleges, especially those with technical programs, are offering courses and degrees in technical communication. Some companies ask for degrees, some for years of experience. There are constant debates on which path to take. Getting low-paying jobs and building up real-world experience is an option some people can't afford without a second income in the family. You can work part-time, doing freelance work from home to build experience or take classes at night. This shows potential employers that you are willing to work at your craft.

"Brush up on your grammar and punctuation skills: take a class in editing. Post your name to do ghostwriting or editing at a local college. Join Internet newsgroups or mailing lists that will give you ideas. Many of these post job opportunities. You won't be ready for most of the jobs at the beginning, but read the postings carefully, along with all job listings on the various newspapers and job websites. Find ones you would like to do someday and read the qualifications. Determine how you can get experience in those areas to someday qualify for your dream job.

"Like other freelance-type jobs, write whenever and whatever you can. Volunteer to do work for any organization or church you might belong to. Tell everyone you meet what you do and what you're looking for. Take a chance whenever you can.

"Here's an example. A woman contacted me through a copyediting list when she learned I was a technical writer. She was in the process of changing careers and knew a little about Web design from what she had learned on her own. She belonged to a riding club and had offered to help design the club's website. A man who owned a small software firm was also a member of the club and offered to sponsor the site. As they talked and worked together, she told him she wanted to be a technical writer. He offered her a freelance job revising a training manual. She asked for my critique of her work and some guidance with revisions. I helped her and saw the drastic improvement in the document. The man was so impressed, he offered her a full-time position.

"When you get that job, learn everything you can. Offer to learn the new applications so you can teach the others in the group, then put the new application and the ability to teach on your resume.

"Offer to take a programming course with the developers so you can learn to read the code and write the manuals and technical installation documents they need—and then put the programming language on your resume.

"Join STC (Society for Technical Communication). That will allow you to post their membership plaque in your work area to let others know you're serious about your profession. It is well worth the yearly dues, and many companies will pay them for you.

"Get permission to submit your best manual to an STC competition. Everything you do and accomplish should go on your resume.

"Every professional should have an updated resume and sample pages at all times. You never know when a company will downsize and you'll be out looking for another job.

"Enjoy the benefits and take the risks. I was the first one to volunteer when many years ago a company I was working for sold an application to a bank in Hong Kong. The bank wanted the software customized for them, and that included the documentation. I was lucky enough to spend nearly a year in Hong Kong, with an apartment, utilities, and a *per diem* paid by the client. You never know where a solid, portable skill such as technical writing can take you."

FINAL WORDS OF ADVICE

Three tips to keep in mind:

1. Be prepared to work hard to learn a variety of applications.

2. To gain experience, volunteer or participate in internships.

3. Once in the door, go that extra mile and learn more than the job requires.

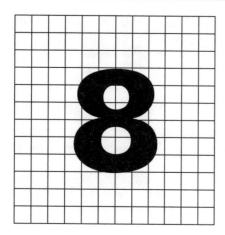

MARKETING, ADVERTISING, AND PUBLIC RELATIONS WRITING

"Most writers regard the truth as their most valuable possession, and therefore are most economical in its use."

—Mark Twain

These three fields—marketing, advertising, and public relations—use the written word as the backbone of their enterprises. To the uninitiated, these three areas might seem to be more similar to each other than not, but there are distinct differences:

- **Marketing** writers are hired to help create a "concept"—the initial introduction to the client's message—and marketing strategy, and then use the written word to communicate that concept to specific audiences.

- **Advertising** copywriters craft advertising copy for use by publications or broadcast media (radio and TV) to promote the sale of goods and services. They work closely with marketing personnel.

- **Public Relations** writers must avoid much of the hype that is freely allowed to advertising writers. While an ad writer can sing the praises of a product or company, a PR writer must get the message across more subtly. Companies pay to have their advertisements run; PR writers try to place stories and press releases as features and editorials, not as advertisements.

Let's have a more in-depth look at each of these three areas.

MARKETING AND ADVERTISING

Although advertising and marketing are distinct fields, they are often linked together. (Some definitions peg marketing as the broad category that encompasses advertising as well as other disciplines, such as public relations and sales.) In simple terms, advertisers create a package to sell a product, service, or idea; marketing experts help decide toward which audiences the advertisement should be aimed.

The goal of advertising and marketing is to reach the consumer—to motivate or persuade a potential buyer; to sell a product, service, idea, or cause; to gain political support; or to influence public opinion. In the words of the American Association of Advertising Agencies (known as the 4 *A*s):

"Advertising is an indispensable part of our economic system. It is the vital link between businesses and consumers.

"The business of advertising involves marketing objectives and artistic ingenuity. It applies quantitative and qualitative research to the creative process. It is the marriage of analysis and imagination, of marketing professional and artist.

"Advertising is art and science, show business and just plain business, all rolled into one. And it employs some of the brightest and most creative economists, researchers, artists, producers, writers, and businesspeople in the country today."

To aid in the advertising endeavor, marketing professionals poll public opinion and analyze the demographics and buying patterns of specific audiences. They play the role of researcher, statistician, social psychologist, and sociologist.

With an idea of the specific audience to target, advertising professionals assess the competition, set goals and a budget, design an advertisement—whether a simple three-line ad or a full-blown campaign—and determine what vehicle is best utilized to reach that audience.

JOB TITLES

Although within smaller agencies, departments can be combined or services contracted out to independent subcontractors, most advertising agencies are organized into the following departments: agency management, account management, creative services, traffic control and production, media services, publicity and public relations, sales promotion, direct response, television production, and personnel.

To work within these departments, advertising agencies employ a number of professionals to perform a variety of duties. Selected job titles are described here.

Agency Manager

In a small agency, the manager could be the president, the owner, or a partner. In giant agencies, the manager could be the chief executive officer reporting to a board of directors or an executive committee, in much the same way any corporation functions. The agency manager is responsible for establishing policies and planning, developing, and defining goals to ensure growth and economic viability.

Account Manager/Executive

An agency's client is usually called an *account*. The account manager supervises all the activity involved with a specific account and is ultimately responsible for the quality of service the client receives.

The account manager functions as a liaison between the advertising agency and the client's organization. He or she must be thoroughly familiar with the client's business, the consumer, the marketplace, and all the aspects of advertising such as media, research, creative design, and commercial production.

Small agencies might function with just one account manager; large mega-agencies could have hundreds or thousands, each handling a multitude of accounts. Account managers usually reach their position after working up through the ranks.

Assistant Account Manager/Executive

Commonly, the assistant account manager reports directly to an account manager and can be assigned a wide range of duties. Some of these duties include analyzing the competition, writing reports, and coordinating creative, media, production, and research projects.

Candidates for this position should possess at least a bachelor's degree, but a specific major in advertising or marketing is not a prerequisite. Communications majors are highly regarded.

Account management departments, along with media departments, hire the greatest number of entry-level candidates. Entry-level positions within the field of advertising often quickly lead to more senior roles.

Creative/Art Director

The creative department of an advertising agency develops the ideas, images, words, and methods that contribute to the ultimate product—the commercial, ad, or campaign. Within an agency's creative department a host of different professionals work together to meet the needs of the client. The art director works with writers, artists, and producers from first conceptualizing the advertisement to its final production.

Entry into the creative department of an advertising agency as a copywriter, designer, or assistant art director is particularly competitive. Having a good portfolio to present to the art director will be a plus. Submitting freelance work can also help you get a foot in the door.

Assistant/Junior Art Director

The assistant art director reports to one or more art directors and is usually responsible for preparing paste-ups and layouts for television storyboards and print ads. The assistant can also be involved in developing visual concepts and designs and supervising commercial production and photo sessions.

Employers expect job candidates to have at least a two-year associate's degree from an art or design school, but they appreciate a bachelor's-level graduate with communication skills and strong graphic arts experience. Even more important, though, is being able to show a top quality portfolio that displays skill and creativity.

The 4 As reports that entry-level opportunities in art departments are very limited for those without some related experience such as an internship or practicum spent in a retail advertising department or another related setting.

Copywriter and Assistant/Junior Copywriter

Copywriters write body copy for print advertising and develop promotional materials. Assignments could range from creating names for companies and products to writing television commercial dialogue or scripts for radio spots, to writing copy for direct-mail packages. Junior copywriters assist the copywriter as well as edit and proofread.

Although a bachelor's degree is not required—a strong portfolio could beat out a degree-holder—majors that are sought after are communications, English, journalism, advertising, or marketing. Even though some of the largest advertising agencies offer copywriting training programs, opportunities are limited for those with no writing experience.

Print Production Manager and Assistant

Personnel in the print production department are responsible for the final creation of the advertisement. After the creative team has specified the different elements it wants incorporated into an ad, the print production team must see to it that the instructions are followed. They are responsible for two-color, four-color, and black and white printing, color separations, and the preparation of mechanicals.

The print production department works closely with the traffic department and the creative staff, and it is also responsible for quality control.

Some experience with production work is the usual requirement to enter this department. Not considered a highly competitive area, it is still a good place for someone to break in and move up.

Assistant Media Planner

The media department is responsible for making sure the advertising is presented to the right audiences, at the right time, and at the right place. As mentioned earlier, media departments are usually open to hiring entry-level candidates.

The assistant media planner reports to a senior planner. His or her usual duties are as follows:

- Gather and study information about people's viewing and reading habits

- Evaluate programming and editorial content of different media vehicles

- Calculate reach and frequency for specific target groups and campaigns

- Become completely familiar with the media in general

- Become completely familiar with specific media outlets

- Become completely familiar with media data banks and information and research sources

Media Buyer

Media buyers and their assistants keep track of where and when print space and air time are available for purchase. They verify that agency orders actually appear or run and calculate costs and rates. They are familiar with all media outlets and are skilled at negotiations.

Other skills media buyers possess include the ability to work under pressure, excellent communication skills, and strong general business skills. They are also adept at working with numbers and are familiar with basic computer programs such as spreadsheet software.

Candidates for entry-level positions are expected to have earned a four-year degree. Some of the large agencies offer training programs for new hires.

Traffic Manager and Assistant

People working in the traffic department make sure that various projects are conceived, produced, and placed as specified. This department is in charge of scheduling and recordkeeping. The traffic department is an excellent place to get a foothold for those with more interest than experience.

Market Researcher

Professionals working in market research departments are tuned in to the consumer—what he or she worries about, desires, thinks, believes, and holds dear. Market researchers conduct surveys or one-on-one interviews, utilize existing research, test consumer reactions to new products or advertising copy, track sales figures and buying trends, and become overall experts on consumer behavior.

Agency research departments can design questionnaires or other methods for studying groups of people, implement the surveys, and interpret the results. Sometimes research departments hire an outside market-research firm to take over some of the workload. For example, a market researcher could come up with a procedure to test the public's reaction to a television commercial; the outside firm would put the procedure into action.

Assistant Research Executive

Assistants report directly to a research executive and are responsible for compiling and interpreting data and monitoring the progress of research projects.

An entry-level assistant research executive has strong quantitative skills and an aptitude for analyzing data. In addition, computer skills and effective writing and speaking skills are a must.

In this field a bachelor's degree is the basic requirement, but it is becoming more and more common to find master's degree and Ph.D. holders. A graduate of a college program that emphasizes research would have an edge on the competition.

Publicists and PR People

While advertising is written exactly the way the client wants and is placed where he or she hopes it will have the most impact, publicity—its wording and placement—is determined by the staff of the media (TV and radio stations, newspapers, etc.) to which it is sent. All media outlets have the option to rewrite press releases or even ignore them. When used properly, however, publicity provides free advertising for products, services, and events.

When it comes to promotion, clients and business owners have more control. They stage events, organize activities, and print and distribute promotional materials.

Here are a few examples of the way publicity and promotion work:

• A sports figure endorses a brand of athletic shoe (for a fee, of course).

- A television talk-show host invites the author of a new book to be a guest on the program.

- A publisher arranges a book-signing tour to promote an author's new book.

- A model demonstrates the features of a yacht at a boat show.

- A soap opera star signs autographs on a tour of shopping malls.

- A professional association imprints its name and logo on tote bags to be given away at the annual conference.

- A company writes and distributes its annual financial report.

- A political candidate reads a ghostwritten speech at a rally.

- A television magazine show explores a breakthrough cure for cancer.

- A vacation resort entices travel writers to visit.

- A beer company sponsors "BeerFest" at a sporting event.

- A "guerrilla marketer" stands on the street corner and thrusts free samples of a product into the hands of passersby.

- Someone wearing a Big Bird outfit stands in front of a shop, inviting passersby to enter.

Those in charge of organizing these promotional activities are called publicists or PR people. They work in a variety of settings and have a wide range of duties. The most important thing they have in common is that they are all excellent communicators. They are also creative and have extensive knowledge of and contact with the media.

PUBLIC RELATIONS

Public relations specialists serve as advocates for businesses, governments, universities, hospitals, schools, and other organizations and strive to build and maintain positive relationships with the public. As managers recognize the growing importance of good public relations to the success of their organizations, they increasingly rely on public relations specialists for advice on strategy and policy of such programs.

Public relations specialists handle such organizational functions as media, community, consumer, and governmental relations; political campaigns; interest-group representation; conflict mediation; or employee and investor relations. However, public relations is not simply "telling the organization's story." Understanding the attitudes and concerns of consumers, employees, and various other groups is also a vital part of the job. To improve communications, public relations specialists establish and maintain cooperative relationships with representatives of community, consumer, employee, and public-interest groups as well as those in print and broadcast journalism.

Those who work in public relations put together information that keeps the general public, interest groups, and stockholders aware of an organization's policies, activities, and accomplishments. Their work keeps management aware of public attitudes and concerns of the many groups and organizations it must deal with.

The public relations department prepares press releases and contacts people in the media who might print or broadcast their material. Many radio or television special reports, newspaper stories, and magazine articles start at the desks of public relations specialists. Sometimes the subject is an organization and its policies toward its employees or its role in the community. Often the subject is a public issue, such as health, nutrition, energy, or the environment.

Public relations specialists also arrange and conduct programs for contact between organization representatives and the public. For example, they set up speaking engagements and often prepare the speeches for company officials. These specialists represent employers at community projects; make film, slide, or other visual presentations at meetings and school assemblies; and plan conventions. In addition, they are responsible for preparing annual reports and writing proposals for various projects.

In government, public relations specialists—who might be called press secretaries, information officers, public affairs specialists, or communications specialists—keep the public informed about the activities of government agencies and officials. For example, public affairs specialists in the Department of Energy keep the public informed about the proposed lease of offshore land for oil exploration. A press secretary for a member of Congress keeps constituents aware of their elected representative's accomplishments.

People who handle publicity for an individual or who direct public relations for a small organization may deal with all aspects of the job. They contact people, plan and do research, and prepare material for distribution. They may also handle advertising or sales promotion work to support marketing.

Some public relations specialists work a standard thirty-five- to forty-hour week, but unpaid overtime is common. In addition, schedules often have to be rearranged to meet deadlines, deliver speeches, attend meetings and community activities, and travel out of town. Occasionally they have to be at the job or on call around the clock, especially if there is an emergency or crisis.

IN-HOUSE OR FREELANCE

Writers in marketing, advertising, and public relations have a choice: work in-house for an agency or firm as a full-time employee or build up a client list and work as a freelancer. You'll see from the first-hand accounts at the end of this chapter that most freelancers have gained a solid background by working first for advertising or PR firms before striking out on their own.

As in any field, there are advantages and disadvantages to both situations. Full-time employees have the security of a regular paycheck but not much say in the projects they must work on. Freelancers have to scramble for new clients, at least when first starting out, and never know exactly how much money they'll earn from month to month. On the other hand, once established, freelancers can pick and choose the projects that interest them.

For those seeking full-time employment, the following section will be of interest.

POSSIBLE EMPLOYERS

Advertising Agencies

About one third of America's advertising professionals work for ad agencies. Approximately 9,600 advertising agencies nationwide employ an estimated 106,000 people. One third are small, one-person offices; another third employ from two to five people; and the remaining third include international mega-companies, such as Young & Rubicam, which has 4,000 employees in thirty-five offices across the United States and close to 3,000 employees in ninety-one foreign countries.

New York continues to be the advertising hub of the world with, according to *Advertising Age*, 61 of the top 100 agencies (ranked by gross income) headquartered there.

But you don't have to move to New York to find work. As mentioned above, many agencies have regional and international offices, and almost every major city, and even smaller ones, can claim its share of agencies.

Advertising agencies help clients, the advertisers, to identify potential customers, create effective advertisements, and arrange for the air time or print space to run the advertising.

Large agencies generally have a wide range of clients and can provide a new graduate with varied work experience. Starting off in a small agency would allow graduates to quickly specialize in a particular area of advertising.

Marketing Firms/Departments

Marketers and advertising professionals work hand in hand, and thus many marketing departments are located within corporate advertising departments or within private advertising agencies. Private marketing firms function similarly to advertising agencies and work toward the same goals—identifying and targeting specific audiences that will be receptive to specific products, services, or ideas.

Corporate Advertising Departments

While many corporations utilize the services of outside advertising agencies and marketing firms, just as many, especially the very large ones, operate their own in-house departments. Here, workers create and develop the company's advertising and sales promotion material. For example, a large department store such as Macy's or Bloomingdale's will have its professional staff create catalogs, brochures, newspaper inserts, and flyers, as well as place the regular flow of daily newspaper ads.

Developing this material, especially glossy catalogs, is a big endeavor, requiring the skills of a variety of people; copywriters, art directors, photographers, layout artists, and modeling agencies and models all play a part.

Corporations that do utilize the services of an outside agency might also maintain their own advertising department to function as a liaison between the agency and the client company. Here the responsibilities include ensuring that the advertising being produced meets the company's objectives and is placed in the appropriate media outlets.

Publishing Companies

Large publishing companies, especially those located in New York City, operate publicity departments to promote their authors and their books. Some of the duties of publicists in a publishing house are arranging for point-of-sale material (for example, printed bookmarks) to be made available at bookstores; organizing book tours, including speaking engagements on television and radio shows and book-signing engagements at bookstores and other appropriate outlets; and writing book jacket copy.

Bookstores

More and more bookstores, especially the new "superstores," coordinate events to bring in the customers. This calls for a publicist who can book big name and local authors for speaking and signing engagements, arrange for cookbook authors to give cooking demonstrations, and find other ways to appeal to the tastes of the book-buying public.

Vacation Resorts/Chambers of Commerce

Promoting a vacation spot or a city falls into the realm of a publicist's duties. Publicists working for a vacation resort would produce pamphlets, brochures, press releases, and perhaps video demonstrations of the location's selling points. Their target audience would be travel agents, travel writers and editors, and the vacationing public.

Publicists working for Chambers of Commerce aim their efforts at potential businesses and new residents, as well as vacationers and other visitors.

THE TRAINING YOU'LL NEED

The course of study potential advertising or marketing specialists should pursue has been the issue of some debate. There are those who believe that a straight degree in advertising or marketing is the best preparation, but they are usually shouted down by those who recognize the importance of a broader curriculum.

To some extent, the answer is determined by the career path you intend to pursue. If you are aiming for the title of account manager, courses in marketing, business and finance, and speech are as important as advertising theory. Potential art directors obviously need technical training in drawing, illustration, and graphic design. All are well served, however, by courses in effective communication. The ability to write and speak well is essential.

Although there are no defined standards for entry into a public relations career, a college degree combined with public relations experience, usually gained through an internship, is considered excellent preparation for public relations work.

Many beginners have a college major in public relations, journalism, advertising, or communications. Some firms seek college graduates who have worked in electronic or print journalism. Other employers seek applicants with demonstrated communication skills and training or experience in a field related to the firm's business—science, engineering, sales, or finance, for example.

Creativity, initiative, good judgment, and the ability to express thoughts clearly and simply are essential. Decision making, problem solving, and research skills are also important.

People who choose public relations as a career need an outgoing personality, self-confidence, an understanding of human psychology, and an enthusiasm for motivating people. They should be competitive, yet flexible and able to function as part of a team.

Some organizations, particularly those with large public relations staffs, have formal training programs for new employees. In smaller organizations, new employees work under the guidance of experienced staff members. Beginners often maintain files of material about company activities, scan newspapers and magazines for appropriate articles to clip, and assemble information for speeches and pamphlets.

After gaining experience, they write news releases, speeches, and articles for publication, or they might design and carry out public relations programs. Public relations specialists in smaller firms generally get all-around experience, whereas those in larger firms tend to be more specialized.

The Public Relations Society of America accredits public relations specialists who have at least five years of experience in the field and have passed a comprehensive six-hour examination (five hours written, one hour oral). The International Association of Business Communicators also has an accreditation program for professionals in the communications field, including public relations specialists. Those who meet all the requirements of the program earn the designation Accredited Business Communicator. Candidates must have at least five years of experience in a communication field and pass a written and oral examination. They also must submit a portfolio of work samples demonstrating involvement in a range of communication projects and a thorough understanding of communication planning. Employers consider professional recognition through accreditation a sign of competence in this field, and it may be especially helpful in a competitive job market.

CAREER OUTLOOK

There are more than 9,600 advertising agencies in the United States, but the 4 As estimates that the number of openings for new grads is only 1,000 to 1,200 each year.

Marketing, advertising, and public relations managers hold about 432,000 jobs in the United States in virtually every industry. Employment is expected to increase faster than the average for all occupations through the year 2006. According to the *Occupational Outlook Handbook*, increasingly intense domestic and global competition in products and services offered to consumers should require greater marketing, advertising, public relations, and promotional efforts. As businesses increasingly hire outside contractors for these services rather than support additional full-time staff, private consulting firms and agencies may experience particularly rapid growth.

Public relations specialists hold about 110,000 jobs nationwide. About two-thirds work in service industries—management and public relations firms, educational institutions, membership organizations, health care organizations, social service agencies, and advertising agencies, for example. Others work for a wide range of employers, including manufacturing firms, financial institutions, and government agencies. A few are self-employed.

Public relations specialists are concentrated in large cities in which press services and other communications facilities are readily available and where many businesses and trade associations have their headquarters. Many public relations consulting firms, for example, are in New York, Los Angeles, Chicago, and Washington, D.C. There is a trend, however, for public relations jobs to be dispersed throughout the nation.

Keen competition for public relations jobs will likely continue among recent college graduates with degrees in communications, journalism, public relations, advertising, or a related field, as the number of applicants is expected to exceed the number of job openings.

THE JOB HUNT

As with the corporate world, it's a good idea for a job seeker to become a familiar fixture inside an advertising agency's front reception area. Sending out resumes blindly has never been an effective method for finding a job in just about any profession. It works even less in these settings. The key is having a good portfolio with you, one that you can quickly open and display if the right person walks by. A portfolio should showcase your best work. If you are interested in copywriting, visuals are less important than writing samples and a good marketing sense. Aspiring art directors need samples of their work that show their design ability.

Persistence is a trait valued in these fields; showing the same quality in your job search can help pay off.

Here are two tips to help you with your search:

1. Start your job search before you near graduation. Those who arrange internships for themselves have an edge; they have already become familiar faces on the job. When an opening comes up a known commodity (who performed well during an internship) is going to be chosen over an unknown one.

2. Learn as much as you can about the agency or firm you're interested in. In other words, target your prospects.

THE MONEY YOU'LL EARN

Salaried Employees

There are conflicting reports on how much you can make, ranging from peanuts to good 'n' plenty levels. It depends mainly upon the agency and your position. According to a National Association of Colleges and Employers survey, starting salaries for marketing majors average about $29,000; advertising majors, about $27,000. Earnings of some highly experienced copywriters were greater than $150,000.

Creatives tend to make more than anyone else. This is followed by account executives and lastly media planners and buyers. One major agency reports that first-year creatives and account people start at around $25,000 a year, while media planners and buyers usually make in the high teens to low twenties. Advancement can come rapidly and substantially. Top creatives and account people can make close to six figures within five years. On the other hand, there are those who might as well be volunteering their time.

Median annual earnings for salaried public relations specialists range between $35,000 and $50,000. However, starting salaries, especially in New York, are notoriously low. Many newbies in advertising say that they can't live in New York on what they make so they have a lot of roommates or get help from their families.

People working for government, health-care, or nonprofit organizations generally earn less than those working for private, for-profit agencies and corporations.

The way most people increase their salary is to change jobs and hop from agency to agency. It's an industry where relationships and networking are crucial to a new position and more money.

Freelancers

Freelancers have a number of ways they charge for their services. Some quote an hourly rate; others charge a flat fee per project. Some use either method, depending on the project.

Here are some freelance writing areas and the income ranges you can expect:

Advertising copywriters—$50 to $100 an hour, or a monthly retainer of $1,000 to $2,000

Catalog copywriting—$45 to $85 an hour

Direct Mail Packages—$2,500 to $10,000 a project

Radio Advertisements—$50 to $2,000 per spot

For more information on what to charge for different projects, consult the current *Writer's Market* (Writer's Digest Books).

FIRST-HAND ACCOUNT

Joan Camenson
Advertising Copywriter

Joan Camenson has more than twenty years of experience as an advertising copywriter with a specialty in retail advertising. She works for the in-house advertising department for Stage Stores, a large retailer specializing in apparel for men, women, and kids. They have more than 600 stores in twenty-five states, with their corporate headquarters in Houston, Texas.

Joan Camenson has an associate's degree in fashion merchandising from the Fashion Institute of Technology, New York.

Getting Started

"I was majoring in merchandising at the time and chose an elective, advertising copywriting. I loved it and found out I had a definite bent to write. I decided I would pursue this as a career.

"I got my very first job by making cold calls to employers in New York City, where I was residing at the time. The college had a placement office, but since I was switching fields (from merchandising to writing) they refused to give me any assistance. So I was on my own. But I was determined.

"For my current job, I initially responded to an ad for a writer, which ran in the local paper. I interviewed for the position, but I did not get it because it was for a junior writer. Three months later, the copy director called to offer me a senior writer position—her staff senior writer was relocating to another state and she needed someone. I have had that position for three years."

The Realities of the Work

"I do retail writing for direct mail catalogs, inserts and statement enclosures, and also newspaper ads. I receive fact sheets from buyers and look at merchandise to come up with copy that will persuade the customers they need to buy this item.

"I attend 'turn-in' meetings, during which the merchants present what they've bought for a particular season or an ad.

"It is busy most of the time. I try to stay current on trends, and I rely on trade papers and the Internet for information.

"I write my ads, then they are corrected by the copy supervisors, and then the ad goes on the board in the form of a proof. When it is in proof form, it shows the copy element (the text) and the photography element. The merchants then approve it or make corrections.

"It's very interesting work because I like fashion and I like to write. I have a lot of interaction with different creative people such as art directors and other writers."

The Upsides and Downsides	"I like the writing and the interaction with the buying staff. The downside is that there are not a lot of retail stores anymore, so opportunities for advancement are limited. I have been trying to get into management here for three years and have not had any luck.

"Also, I wish we had more of a team effort and that there were more discussions on how to work on a particular project."

Earnings	"I earn $37,000, and I feel I should be making more. Part of the problem I can attribute to myself—I should have switched jobs more often. It's a sad state of affairs that companies seem to pay more for someone coming in, but they won't financially reward existing staff personnel, so you only get money when you switch jobs.

"Someone just starting out would probably earn in the mid-twenties, and there would be room for advancement at a lower level. Raises are small; I have averaged around $1,000 to $1,500 a year."

Advice from Joan Camenson	"I would advise people to get as much exposure to different types of writing as they can. My limitations are that I have no experience in media—radio or TV—and this is definitely a mistake.

"I would encourage people to learn as much as they can about print, media, and the Internet. I definitely feel that the Internet is the future. When I started out, there were lots of retail organizations, all with their own advertising departments, and so there were lots of opportunities to find jobs. Today, that is not the case. Stores are swallowing up other stores, and you have a much more limited area to work.

"I would also encourage people to minor in a topic that they like so that they can write about it, if they choose writing/journalism as their major. I remember meeting a nurse who was an editor for a nursing magazine. She had majored in nursing and had a minor in writing. She was able to successfully combine both of her interests. If I had it to do over again, I would have tried to find out about becoming a travel writer or a food writer."

FIRST-HAND ACCOUNT

Marina Richards
Advertising/Marketing Writer

Marina Richards has worked in a variety of advertising agencies as a full-time copywriter, but now she is freelancing. She writes print ads, radio and TV scripts, website content, brochures, and direct response materials.

She has a B.A. in advertising and has been working in the field since 1986.

Getting Started

"I liked the idea of combining my acumen for business with my love for creative writing. And I knew I would get to work with interesting people.

"I got my first job the summer after I'd graduated from college with a degree in advertising. I heard about a writing/editing position that had opened up at my local ABC television affiliate. Everyone and his brother wanted this job, so I didn't think I stood a chance. Fingers shaking, I phoned the director of advertising who was also the hiring manager. She invited me in for an interview. She told me to bring my portfolio. My what?!, I thought, telling her I most certainly would.

"Then I locked myself in my room for a week, scrambling to pull together a portfolio of writing and concepting samples. Everything from college suddenly looked amateurish, stale, old. I can't draw, so I cut photos and other visuals out from magazines and glued them to my art boards. Very neatly. You should have a basic sense for layout and design as a copywriter so you can imagine your concept, and this is what I wanted to show in my portfolio.

"Next, I drew in the headlines with a marker and typed up the body copy, basing my directions on my own marketing strategies. The interview went well because she invited me back for a second visit. Then I met the television general manager and other very important people and was given a tour of the station. Still, when the hiring manager walked me to the door and shook my hand, I had no idea whether I had the job or not. I called her a week later, and she said to call her again in two weeks. Two weeks later, I was on a trip with my parents in California. We stopped along the Pacific Coast Highway to get something to eat. The restaurant hovered over the sea, and bustled with harried waitresses and travelers. I bolted for the pay phone, telling myself to stay calm, it was only a job; a very desirable, prestigious job for a fresh-faced college kid, but it was merely a job. No reason to toss myself over the cliffs if I didn't get it.

"Needless to say, they never found my body at the bottom of those cliffs because I got the job—even with my homemade portfolio!

"After ten years of working in advertising agencies, TV stations, and in-house corporate departments, I went freelance. Now I work from my home office."

The Realities of the Work

"Agencies are notoriously laid back when projects have slowed down. But when projects are hot, you are under pressure and you work to deadline. Sometimes you work around the clock for a very high-profile project or job.

"Say, for example, a client needs a direct response brochure to 'roll-out' (introduce) his latest telecommunications package to business-to-business clients. After the A.E. [Account Executive] has briefed you and the A.D. [Art Director] has been assigned to this project, they give you a marketing strategy. This is your map, your guide as to what to do. It has to be dead on, or you send it back to the A.E.

"The first thing you and the art director do is start 'concepting'—come up with ideas. You'll flip through old design magazines and look over anything from the client's competition, along with materials that were created for any similar products at any time.

"What I like to do is ask clients to show me a campaign they loved. That's a great way to gauge taste. Then, as the writer, you want to know what tone—formal, informal, salesy, highbrow, conversational—the copy should reach for. As a pro, you should be able to write in many different voices. That's very important.

"Your A.E. will be bugging you while you're trying to concentrate, popping her head around the corner every hour with a panicky smile, 'How's it going?'

"Once you've written the copy based on this one concept, the C.D. [Creative Director] will read it over and make some comments, usually very helpful ones. You make the changes.

"You and the A.D. present the visuals and copy to the A.E. and his or her boss. This is a panicky moment. Think politics here. The senior A.E. and the marketing director could be a problem if they don't like your concept.

"If they do, you gab in the hallway about how you're going to present your materials to the client. You may have worked into the next day by now. You've been drinking lots of coffee, and you feel like you've been on the space shuttle.

"The client and his people come to your office. You, the writer, have no idea how many people you're presenting your work to today. There is an art to presenting advertising and marketing ideas, and everyone has his or her own style.

"What usually happens is the A.E. makes a presentation, then introduces you. You pull out the art boards and start talking about the concept. Be interesting. Add value to the client's product. Anticipate questions. Tell them why this concept will work for their strategy. If they don't like the concept, it's back to the drawing board.

"But in this case they do. They loved everything you said. They have requested you, in fact, for all their projects from now on! The meeting was a success. Now you go back to the agency and polish the copy. You may even start coming up with more collateral (brochures, ads, etc.) per your A.E.'s direction to go with the initial roll-out brochure. You are now working on a full-blown campaign. This will take a month or so.

"What's great about being the writer is that you're only involved in this heavy-duty work in the beginning. Production and all that starts later. Your copy is approved, the art director and designer are working it into their layouts, and you have time to go shopping between editing the copy for typos and word changes.

"Next, you get what's called the 'blue-lines.' Here the layout and copy are typeset. Finally, the brochure is out of preproduction and comes to you for one last look. Usually you receive what's called a 'printer's proof,' or just 'proof.' It's mostly for the art director, but the copywriter should see it too because he or she wants to make sure the printer didn't miss a word, or print the brochure backwards.

"And that's it. Your brochure, the baby you've been nurturing, the creative concept that drew from your head and onto paper, is done. When the finished product arrives, you grab a few for your portfolio."

The Upsides and Downsides

"The upside is that you are paid to be creative. That's fun! You get to work with creative and, more often than not, very smart people.

"The best agencies and advertising departments make art. The copy sings, and the visuals dance in sync with the strategy.

"You could get famous, too. And you could win awards. The bottom line, however, is that you must be able to write like a dream. It's one of the most competitive fields in business today.

"The downsides are that so many things can go wrong, the client might not like your concept, and the pressure might be overwhelming."

Earnings

"My salary at a Boston ad agency was $62,000 a year. I was a copywriter for a very large agency. A senior writer would make more, but it depends on where you work. Now my fee as a freelancer is usually based on an hourly rate of $60 to $75 per hour, depending on the project."

Advice from Marina Richards

"You should be innovative, be able to think for yourself, and don't be afraid to ask questions.

"You should have a sense of irony, creatively speaking, but hokey or cornball humor is not what creative directors and others look for.

"You must be able to write and come up with smart ideas. You don't have to be brilliant, but you should make others think you are!

"Go to school and get a B.A. in English, advertising, history, communications, or journalism. Make contacts, write great letters, catch someone's attention, get interviews, come back for more interviews, show off your portfolio, make them like you personally, get hired.

"It can be a cutthroat business. But once you have enough experience, you can take your samples and go just about anywhere and make a living."

FIRST-HAND ACCOUNT

Susan Ditz
Public Relations Writer

Susan Ditz is the owner of SMD Communications, a marketing communications, public relations, and editorial services concern in California. She writes applications, trend and success stories, newsletter pieces, and Web content, in addition to press kit materials such as fact sheets, backgrounders, white papers, and brochures. She also writes company and executive profiles that she places in the Business Journal, and she ghostwrites features for executives. She also works as a contractor for several PR agencies on special projects. She has a B.S. in journalism from Boston University and has been working in the field since 1973.

Getting Started

"This field really chose me—out of necessity. After graduating I went to work for a weekly newspaper group in Massachusetts as assistant editor. When the paper was sold, I was in a bit of a panic about money, so I did some temping as a secretary—I was a miserable failure.

"Someone had told me about a little agency in town that needed help. I talked my way into a job as an account executive by stretching the truth about my PR training at BU—which was nil. My boss was fairly desperate for an assistant because he'd landed a major new account. He was one part P. T. Barnum and one part Walter Winchell, who sounded like Paul Harvey and liked that I had newspaper experience. He was a fixture in Worcester, Massachusetts, and a PR guy from the Edward Bernays school. He taught me how to write a proper press release, develop a television script, produce a TV show, write an advertorial, and manage events.

"I quickly learned I could make more in PR than as a junior staffer on a paper, so I went on to a bigger agency in Boston, where I worked on PR for McDonald's, Nabisco, PUCH Mopeds, and Dexter Shoe. In addition to press kits, I prepared cause-related marketing materials and wrote newsletters and brochures.

"After working in the agency, corporate and nonprofit sectors, I started consulting in 1985. I was a single mother, and I wanted to have a much more flexible schedule and to stop commuting."

The Realities of the Work

"*Diverse* is a good description. Over the years I've had clients in health care, nonprofit, computer software, hardware and peripherals, telecommunications, wine and food, restaurants, shoes, bicycles, real estate, marine products, and sporting goods. Currently, I am writing content for a website, developing two feature stories, preparing a marketing plan for a nonprofit group, and planning long-range publicity for several entertainers.

"My days are always full of deadlines. Really effective PR depends on being proactive and innovative. I need to scan industry publications and websites to stay on top of emerging trends or potential problems. I get a lot of ideas this way.

"A large part of what I do at the beginning of each day is strategic management—making decisions and setting priorities. Then I spend the rest of the day executing my plan, developing tomorrow's plan, and trying to stay on top of E-mail. The day doesn't end until the work is finished—typically my day is twelve hours with lunch at my desk.

"I write on assignment and develop my own ideas. Opportunities come along daily; so does new business.

"Being on my own requires that I be a pretty good juggler. It is not uncommon for me to have four to six projects in process at a time. I like it that way; it's never boring. Recently, however, I spent about two months working eighty-hour weeks with almost no breaks because a contract job lasted way beyond the original deadline and I had already committed to do a lesser paying project.

"Being a consultant is not for the faint of heart. I've had months where projects got stalled so no money was coming in. These are the times I start buying lottery tickets, or wishing I'd gone to law school. It usually gets me looking furiously at websites and classified ads for a full-time position. But then the phone rings and I'm taking notes for a proposal."

The Upsides and Downsides

"There is a lot of potential for very interesting adventures—a chance to learn something new and work with bright, creative people.

"But there's lots of stress, and a considerable level of frustration, working with the media and keeping up with communication technology."

Earnings

"I earn in the mid-to-high five figures, depending on the year. Being a PR consultant is not a way to get rich. Starting salaries vary, depending on where you are in the country. Salaries in Silicon Valley, where I am, are high, but so is the exorbitant cost of living."

Advice from Susan Ditz

"While you're a student, take advantage of every opportunity to intern in agencies, nonprofits, and corporations. Before embarking on a PR career, get some experience working in the news business. If you think you want to work in the corporate world, do so for awhile before investing in an M.B.A. And read a lot."

FIRST-HAND ACCOUNT

Newman Mallon
Public Relations Writer

Newman Mallon is a self-employed public relations consultant and writer. His company is called Media Insight and is based in Toronto, Ontario.

He earned a Bachelor of Applied Arts in radio and television arts from Ryerson Polytechnical Institute in Toronto, and a Bachelor of Journalism from Carleton University in Ottawa.

He has been in this field a total of eighteen years, six years on his own as a freelancer.

Getting Started

"After studying radio and television arts, I worked for five years as an audiovisual technician for a school board. This was good training ground, but I noticed a lot of PR or media relations jobs in the newspaper that required a journalism degree. Having taken three radio and TV writing courses at Ryerson, I realized I enjoyed writing, and I decided to take a one-year program in journalism at Carleton for university grads with a good writing portfolio, thus building on my previous degree.

"I got my first related job because of a referral from a professor at Carleton to my then boss, who was a previous journalism grad.

"I was later able to get into a self-employment program sponsored by the unemployment insurance commission, which supplied a weekly living allowance to start my own business."

The Realities of the Work

"The writing I do is largely high-tech as well as industrial, financial, and business-to-business. Projects include corporate backgrounders, speeches, press releases, PR planning, and feature and ghostwritten articles.

"In most agencies, PR writers are named account executives and therefore are liaisons to the client. They write the copy for press releases, corporate backgrounders, feature articles, speeches, and proposals as well. In an agency that also offers integrated marketing communications, the PR writer may also write brochures, invitations, mailers, moving notices, or even audiovisual presentations.

"The clients you'll work with will vary from agency to agency. If the agency specializes in high tech, you may find yourself working on business software in the morning and computer games in the afternoon. If it's a consumer-related agency, it could be hair mousse one hour and motorcycles the next. Consulting, PR planning, idea or story angle development, research, writing, revisions, and approvals are all part of the job.

"Mostly you will have to come up with your own ideas for editorial pieces that will suit the publication. This means they must be informative or interesting to readers of the publication. Unlike advertising, where you can play up the client and products, editorial material should be done without much hype about the company you are working for. Basically, a mention of its name, a review of its product, a business success story, or some quotes from a spokesperson is what you are after. This keeps the company name in the news. Accolades about the company will not be printed, so go into ad copywriting if you like to write powerful, compelling copy.

"When you are doing your planning to determine what editors or publications you could approach, you first look for magazines that go to the client's target audience or decision makers who might buy the company's product. Then you look for editorial features that have something to do with the product or industry, and you develop a story or informative piece to fit that feature issue. Then you call or E-mail the editor with a proposal or pitch. Often, the publication will want its own staff writers to actually write the piece. If that's so, great. Set up any interviews they need and provide them with information about the company. If you will be writing it, discuss it with the editor so you know what he or she wants.

"The job can be very hectic, trying to find new clients, pitch stories to editors, and research and write articles or news releases that editors will print. Often, clients do not understand you have to write for the editor or it will not be printed. This requires a lot of hand-holding and explanation to clients who are new to PR. Clients also do not realize how long it takes to pitch and write a good editorial piece.

"Since I own my own business, about 60 percent of my time is spent on administrative details and marketing my own services. The rest is writing/consulting or billable work. If your dream is to start your own business, be prepared for ups and downs when it is overstimulating for awhile, and then just tough-slogging on the phone, trying to get other clients.

"Many people think you can take time off any time you want if you have your own business. Well, dream on. In your own business you might get to choose what fifty-five hours of the week you'd like to work, but often this is not possible since you have ten bosses instead of just one. Maybe once you hire several people and can afford a very good vice president, then you can take time off."

Earnings

"Someone starting out in public relations can probably expect about $20,000 per year, rising to about $50,000 as a senior consultant. The salary can go higher if you should reach the director or V.P. level."

Advice from Newman Mallon

"To get started, get whatever experience you can by writing for smaller publications, and then work your way up to develop a portfolio. This will display you can write for the press. Any experience helps find that first job and gives you an advantage over someone else, even if it's volunteer work for a charity.

"Of course, good written and verbal communication skills are mandatory. You should also be diplomatic and able to work well on your own as well as in a team environment.

"Knowledge of a specific industry you've worked in previously will also help you land that first job, if your prospective employer has a client in that industry."

FIRST-HAND ACCOUNT

Bob Mansker
Deputy Public Printer of the United States

Bob Mansker has worked for many years as a press secretary for Congressman Martin Frost from Texas. He holds an M.B.A and Ph.D. in business administration.

Getting Started

"I always had a fascination with reporters—but a lack of desire to follow the traditional journalism track, working for newspapers or television and radio. This, coupled with my interest in politics, provided the perfect background for a career as a press secretary.

"I started volunteering for local political campaigns. I wrote press releases and newsletters, and I became familiar with the political process, keeping on top of current events and making a lot of contacts. When Congressman Martin Frost, Democrat from Texas, won his first seat in the House of Representatives in 1979, he moved to Washington, and I moved with him.

"When I was involved with political campaigning and during a stint in the state legislature, I gained an insight into the needs—written and verbal, radio and television press—of a political organization. I learned how to write press releases and newsletters for various members of Congress."

The Realities of the Work

"I write press releases on the Congressman's position on a multitude of issues. These releases are then sent to different media—newspapers, TV, radio, etc.— with the hopes that the information will be printed or aired.

"I also write a weekly newspaper column and produce *Martin Frost Reports*, a monthly newsletter on a variety of issues for the voters in the district. I produce radio and television programs, scheduling the Congressman in various studios. I also meet regularly with media representatives from various newspapers and magazines, television and radio.

"About three or four times a year I travel to and from the congressional district in Texas to remain acquainted with local media. And occasionally I get to travel abroad: I went on a trip to Russia a few years ago, for example, accompanying the Congressman, and recently I visited the Middle East—Syria, Saudi Arabia, and the United Arab Emirates."

The Upsides and Downsides

"I interact with individuals who are constantly keeping aware of national and world events and who have a respect for the political structure and makeup of the political electorate of the nation.

"Also, I get to bring my beagle, Vicky, to work. I have a new office that's out of the way a bit, and I'm the staff director, so no one minds.

"The job depends on the Congressman deciding to seek reelection and being reelected. Every two years we have to revisit the issue. You work strictly at his decision.

"Fortunately, Congressman Frost does plan to continue seeking reelection; he says he's in for the long term.

"If the time ever comes, with the contacts I've made, I could move to another office. Or, I would be equally content to go back to teaching. Before I became a press secretary, I taught business and real estate at various universities in my home state.

"The only other downside is that sometimes it does get repetitious to a degree, but what job doesn't?"

Advice from Bob Mansker

"A college degree is not really necessary for a career as a press secretary. If someone was in tune with the operation and had a good grasp of the English language and a knowledge of the home state, he or she could be hired. But, basically, you'd wonder why he or she hadn't gone to college. Having the degree would give an edge on any job and it shows stamina, an ability to complete a task.

"Having said that, practical experience campaigning is better than a degree in political science, for example. But a major in general communications would be an advantage.

"Writing and organizational abilities are crucial. So is the ability to type. And an all-around good press secretary needs some understanding of radio, television, and newspapers.

"If you come to apply for one of these positions, we aren't just going to look at your writing or journalism ability. We're going to look at you as a person."

FIRST-HAND ACCOUNT

Marcus Grimm
Radio Copywriter

Marcus Grimm worked for three years in Hershey, Pennsylvania, as the production coordinator for WRKZ-FM, a 50,000-watt country station. He wrote everything from advertising copy to press releases, corporate video scripts to newsletters.

He has a B.A. in communications from Elizabethtown College in Elizabethtown, Pennsylvania.

Getting Started

"As someone who has always loved radio, and always loved writing, radio copywriting was the one job that allowed me to blend my two interests.

"I got my job in a roundabout way. In a college professional-writing class, I had an assignment to interview someone doing a job that I would like to do. I called the largest local radio station and got an interview with the creative director. After I finished my interview, I gave him a copy of it, and he was impressed with my portrayal of him. I volunteered to do some writing for him. After being a volunteer, I used the same radio station for an internship, and by the time I finished my internship, more than a year later, my boss couldn't remember working without me, so I was offered a paying job to do the same work."

The Realities of the Work

"At our radio station there were about twelve different sales representatives. Each one would bring in a copy sheet, which detailed what the client was trying to sell on the radio. If the clients had an idea about how they wanted their company or products portrayed, it would be indicated there. Often, they might just indicate tone—for example, 'no funny ads,' or 'client would love to see funny ideas.'

"From there, I would write the script and have someone voice and produce the spot. Then, I would either play the spot over the phone for the client or give a cassette copy to the sales rep to play for the client in person.

"The clients were extremely varied, ranging from lawyers and optometrists to car dealers, tractor dealers, and farmer's market owners.

"Virtually everything I wrote was sixty-second scripts. Some radio commercials are thirty seconds, but most stations charge the same amount for a thirty as a sixty, as research has shown that it is the quantity of commercials (not length) that causes someone to change stations. Some scripts focused on making people aware of what the advertiser does, while others would highlight special products or sales.

"For example, 'H&H Tack Shop is having the following sale this month . . . ,' or 'Visit Dr. X and never wear glasses again.'

"Although the subject matter was, of course, up to the client, the theme of the ad was usually up to me, and it is the choice of theme that will render your ad good or bad.

"Radio stations are exciting places to work. It is an instant medium, and advertisements may literally air within minutes of being written and produced.

"I also think that it's a great 'crutch' system to develop writing skills. Very often I've found that I won't write a story because I can't form all of the elements properly. In radio copywriting, most of the elements are provided for you (characters, setting, etc.), but you must fill in the blanks. Because radio is 'the theater of the mind,' there are no rules. One time I wrote an ad about a truck driving through a wall of eggs! In television, this would have been an expensive proposition. In radio, it was free.

"Radio stations also offer occasional glimpses into celebrity lives. Musicians coming into town to play concerts often stop by radio stations to thank them for playing their recent releases.

"At our radio station, I never worked more than forty hours per week, but that was mainly because my creative director was a real pro at effective writing. I learned to write copy quickly and effectively. More than once he told me, 'This isn't *War and Peace*, it's a radio ad! Cut it down.' And I did."

The Upsides and Downsides

"I always loved the wide variety of personalities in radio. They are truly some of the most creative, intelligent people I have had the pleasure of being around. I also enjoyed the wide variety of writing styles I got to practice daily.

"Another upside is that intangible appreciation you feel when you hear your own commercial over the airwaves.

"The greatest downside to working in radio copywriting is the money, which inevitably drove me out of the business. Unfortunately, copywriting is considered to be an expense in radio (as are on-air personalities). As an expense, the station did whatever possible to keep the pay low.

"The only other downside is understanding that, in the end, the commercial is owned by the client. This means that no matter how wonderful or inventive your idea is, if the client doesn't love it, the idea won't go anywhere."

Earnings

"Again, I got into radio by offering my services for free, and if you have the ability, that's probably the easiest way to get in, as it's a very competitive business. Eventually I was paid $6 per hour. The day I decided to get out of radio was when I found out that after twenty years in the business, the creative director at our station was making only $28,000 per year.

"In the radio business, pay is often relative to station and market size, and I was working for the largest station in our market. Since I wasn't looking to move, I realized that my pay would not likely ever exceed my boss's."

Advice from Marcus Grimm

"Volunteer. Volunteer. Volunteer. It's the best way to get into the environment and see what radio is all about. If I were going into the business today, I would spend some time listening to commercials from different stations, to see which are the most creative. Some copywriters are lightyears ahead of others.

"As far as writing is concerned, true artists will be less happy in this field, because the client's desires must always come before your own.

"Ideally, you must be someone who can appreciate the necessity of business, and only then can you spin a creative tale around it. You must be able to handle criticism, which will come from clients and salespeople.

"Finally, understand that unless you're happy making less than average money, radio copywriting will probably serve as an extremely enjoyable stepping stone to an advertising agency or more lucrative position elsewhere. Still, appreciate it for what it is.

"In the words of my old boss, 'Radio is the ultimate dream world. We've got cowboys that never rode a horse and guitar players who never held a pick.'"

FINAL WORDS OF ADVICE

To make a successful career for yourself as an advertising, marketing, or PR writer, keep these three tips in mind:

1. While many writers (novelists, nonfiction book writers, article writers) come up with their own ideas and are free to pursue them, writers in these fields work for clients who have their own ideas. You must be willing and able to write in a variety of styles and on a range of topics, depending on the needs of the client.

2. Though self-employment may be your ultimate goal, be willing to work at an agency, even if it means starting at the bottom. This is a wonderful way to get experience and an overall understanding of how the industry works.

3. If you're freelancing, don't be afraid to expand your search for clients outside your own locale. Use the Internet or your library's out-of-state telephone books to locate new business prospects, or place advertisements in related publications to make your services known.

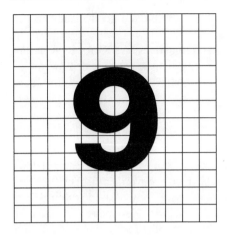

OTHER OPPORTUNITIES FOR WRITERS

"I would sooner read a timetable or a catalogue than nothing at all."

—W. Somerset Maugham

Career writers don't just write books or articles for magazines or newspapers. And there are many avenues to pursue other than technical, advertising, or PR writing. Some permit (or require) full-time employment; others allow for freelancing independence.

Here's a list of writing or writing-related job titles that, in this book, fall under the category of other opportunities for writers:

Agent	Critiquer	Resume Writer
Book Reviewer	Ghostwriter	Speechwriter
Comedy Writer	Greeting Card Writer	Writing Instructor/Lecturer
Contest Judge	Newsletter Writer	
Copyeditor	Reader	

AGENT

Many agents start off in publishing houses as editors, working with a particular genre or two. They go into agenting to have more freedom with the type of books they'll handle. Many agents are also writers and know what the industry is like from both sides of the fence.

Some of the bigger literary agencies, which are mostly in New York City, hire assistants and provide training until you can be promoted to associate status. Agents with more experience in the publishing field might immediately start their own agency after a stint at a publishing house.

Yes, there are agents with no experience who also go out on their own. They have few contacts with publishers, are not familiar with what types of projects the different editors are seeking, and often charge fees to writers for their services, above and beyond the usual commission. Writers are strongly warned to avoid these agents. To be a successful agent, you need to build a good reputation for yourself based on well-earned experience.

Contact the Association for Author's Representatives (AAR) for more information on becoming an agent. Their address and website are provided for you in Appendix A.

BOOK REVIEWER

Most large newspapers and some magazines and newsletters feature book sections. Although many of the book reviews are written by the book section editor or staff writer, some publications will accept freelance work.

To get your foot in the door, you can purchase a copy of a book you would like to review, read it, then write it up, and send it in. Newspapers in different regions of the country do not compete with each other, so you could sell one review to more than one market.

If you make a sale, the next assignment will be easier to come by, and you'll be given a comp copy of the book(s) you are going to review.

Another way to go is to simply query a book editor first, before writing the review. They might provide you with a comp copy or expect you to get your own. If the latter is the case, you can contact the publisher of the book(s) you'd like to review with a request for a review copy. Many publishers are quite generous with their comp copies and ask in return only that you send them a copy of the review when it sees print.

Your query might produce an assignment, or at least an agreement to look at your review on spec. Querying first will also let you know if the book you have chosen has already been reviewed.

COMEDY WRITER

"Take my wife, please . . ." If you can come up with something more original than that, you might find your niche writing comedy routines and gags for stand-up comics or jokes for people who have to speak in front of an audience.

Contact comedians (hang out in comedy clubs and see how approachable they are) or speakers bureaus, and offer your services. The rates you could expect to receive are listed later in this chapter.

CONTEST JUDGE

Most contest judges for well-known writers contests are usually already professional agents, editors, or authors. This is not an area for an unknown to find work.

Judges are usually assigned specific categories, such as short-story entries or romance novels, and then given a number of entries to read, sometimes critique, and judge.

COPYEDITOR

Some publishers rely on the services of freelance copyeditors to proof and mark up manuscripts to get them ready for typesetting and printing. You have to be a stickler for detail to be comfortable with this type of work. You also must be familiar with the type of editorial notations you'd find in *The Chicago Manual of Style*, for example. Approach publishers with a letter and resume.

CRITIQUER

Look in the back pages of any magazine geared toward writers, and you'll see a slew of ads placed by critiquers, manuscript evaluators, and "book doctors." You can place one there, too.

To be a good critiquer you must have an understanding of what makes fiction or nonfiction publishable, know how to point out strengths and weaknesses, have a good command of grammar and structure, and be an articulate report writer.

Good critiquers also know never to promise publication or agent representation upon completion of their critique and a rewrite by the writer. This type of false advertising has had state's attorneys general investigating and punishing these improper practices.

GHOSTWRITER

Ghostwriters write books for people who don't have the necessary skill to do it themselves. The client could be a famous person such as a former president or a movie star who has a story to tell but needs help doing it. Other clients could be self-publishers or experts in a particular field who have topics they want to see in print but don't have the time, skill, or experience to do it themselves.

Ghostwriters sometimes get credit for their writing (you might see "as told to" on the book jacket cover), but many times they stay anonymous, writing behind the scenes.

Landing a ghostwriting job for a celebrity is not an easy task, unless you know someone. Publishers, more often than not, assign these books to writers they have worked with in the past.

But this doesn't mean that a writer with credits to show and some chutzpah couldn't approach a celebrity with a pitch something along these lines: "As a writer interested in [celebrity's specialty], I have faithfully followed your career since [date of the celebrity's first accomplishment]. I know you have a story to tell, and I would love to help you tell it. I haven't seen your autobiography in bookstores yet, but it's a book I know publishers—and the public—would be interested in." Who knows, it could work . . .

Ghostwriting for a self-publisher is the easiest way to get credits for yourself, but pitfalls abound. Often self-publishers have already written a book, but they have had no luck selling it to a publisher. The reason, they are sure, is the short-sightedness of the publisher, not any shortcomings the book may have. They might want you to rewrite the book or add your name as coauthor to lend credibility to the project. You'll get paid when you sell the book.

Or they might have what they consider to be a hot idea—and if only they could write, they know the book would be a bestseller. They want you, the ghostwriter, to write it for them and submit it to publishers, and they will pay you whatever you want—out of the huge advance they're sure the book will merit.

In both situations, most professional writers would say, simply, no. Professionals know how difficult it is to sell a book, and if they are going to have to wait until it sells to be paid, they might as well continue working on their own books.

Contacting book packagers (listed in the *Literary Marketplace*) with your resume, writing samples, and stated availability and areas of expertise could possibly land you a contract. For example, a book packager has just been assigned a travel book on South Africa. You have just come back from a six-month tour there. And your letter—wonder of wonders—happens to arrive just as the packager hangs up the phone and is scratching his head, pondering who he could possibly find for this project. Being in the right place at the right time can go a long way. And it does happen.

GREETING CARD WRITER

"Roses are red, violets are blue . . ." Someone writes those greeting cards and gets paid fairly nicely for such a small number of words. Greeting card publishers usually will look at several ideas at once, buy all rights, and pay either upon acceptance or upon publication. You can find greeting card publishers and information on how to submit to them in the most recent *Writer's Market* (Writer's Digest Books).

NEWSLETTER WRITER

Most organizations, from big-time corporations to small nonprofits and charities, put out newsletters. These can be aimed at a variety of audiences, including staff, members, stockholders, donators, neighborhood residents, clients, customers, and potential customers.

The focus and content of newsletters will vary depending on the audience and activities of the organization putting out the newsletter. They could range from news on the health care industry to stock tips, to a listing of potential markets for freelance writers to approach.

Some newsletters are available at no charge to subscribers and are sent through E-mail or regular post; others charge a subscription fee or depend on advertising—or both—to cover expenses.

Depending on the size and the budget of the organization, some newsletters are generated in-house; others are contracted out to freelance writers and editors.

Newsletter writers might provide all or part of the content, or they might depend upon contributions from staff or other outside freelancers. Some newsletter writers are solely responsible for layout, proofreading, editing, and printing; others report to an editor and work with graphic artists and typesetters.

Writers find jobs writing newsletters through classified ads, through on-line databases, by contacting organizations directly, through word of mouth, and sometimes through internships and by volunteering.

It is rare that one newsletter would provide enough income to support a writer, so most freelancers who specialize in newsletters have contracts with more than one organization, or they do other types of writing in addition.

You'll learn more about being a newsletter writer through a first-hand account later in this chapter. See also Chapter 4 for a breakdown of the article-writing process.

READER

You may have seen advertisements offering you easy money just for reading and screening out books for publishers or agents. The advertiser—for a fee—will show you how to land these plum jobs. The next time you see one of those advertisements, keep turning the pages. Most of these offers are scams. Agents and editors either do their own reading or have junior-level assistants handle it.

RESUME WRITER

Job seekers need resumes and you can find work writing and updating them. Resume writers work for employment agencies, or they freelance, leaving business cards at print shops and advertising in newspapers, career magazines, and on-line.

Resume writers must be familiar with the different resume and curriculum vitae formats. They must also be able to listen to their clients in order to pull out the appropriate information. In addition, they must know how to tailor each resume to the specific type of job being sought.

When working with a new graduate with little or no experience, good resume writers must know how to translate information into *resumese*. For example, "works well as part of a team" is something a resume writer would put down for a job seeker who played basketball or some other team sport in college.

SPEECHWRITER

Speechwriters work with politicians and other public figures, listening to what they want to say, researching the issues, then writing the speeches they will deliver. When you see the president on television or hear the mayor or governor speaking to a group of voters, you can be pretty certain the speech was written by someone else.

Speechwriters find work through word of mouth and contacts, sometimes through classified advertisements, but mostly by volunteering in campaigns and making themselves known and their work stand out.

Speechwriters can be employed full-time for an elected official, or they might follow different candidates over the years from campaign to campaign. They can also be paid by the project.

You'll learn more about being a speechwriter through a first-hand account later in this chapter.

WRITING INSTRUCTOR/LECTURER

The old adage, "those who can, do; those who can't, teach," doesn't apply here. The best writing instructors are those who are good writers themselves and can offer constructive criticism to students.

Writing instructors work in colleges and universities. They also work for adult education programs, or they are hired to speak and conduct workshops for various writers organizations or conferences. Some writing instructors organize their own workshops and seminars, renting classroom or hotel space, or meeting in their own homes. Still others conduct classes on-line, either via E-mail or Internet chat rooms.

To make your services known, take the following steps:

• Conduct an Internet search for on-line (as well as off-line) writing programs

• Contact local writers groups such as state chapters of Romance Writers of America or Mystery Writers of America

• Visit local bookstores and offer to speak on a subject of interest to writers, in addition to sitting for a book-signing

• Contact your local library and offer to do a series of workshops for writers

• Apply to the adult education programs offered by universities, community colleges, and school boards

• Organize your own seminars: rent a mailing list (*Writer's Digest* is a good source), rent a meeting room, decide on topics, print up brochures, and mail them out

THE MONEY YOU'LL EARN

The following table is a breakdown of the payment you can expect for a variety of writing jobs not covered in previous chapters. The information is culled from the *2000 Writer's Market* (Writer's Digest Books) and is updated every year. For a more complete listing, consult the most recent *Writer's Market*.

Table 9.1 Breakdown of wages for various careers

Job Title	*Wages*
Agent	15 percent commission from the sale of their clients' work to publishers; some charge 20 percent for foreign and movie rights
Book reviewer	$35 to $200 and a copy of the book; for small newspapers, a byline and copy of the book
Comedy writer	for nightclub entertainers, $5 to $25 per gag; $100 to $1,000 per minute for routines
Contest judge	$10 per entry for short submissions; up to $500 for overall contest judging, depending on the contest
Copyeditor	freelancing for book publishers, $15 to $75 an hour or $3 to $5 a page
Critiquer	from $2 to $5 per double-spaced page for line notes and report; $15 to $30 an hour for theses/dissertations
Ghostwriter	writing for a celebrity or expert, for a self-published book, or for a publisher, with credit, expect the full advance (typically between $15,000 and $25,000), plus 50 percent of the royalties; hourly rates for self-publishers range from $25 to $85
	no credit, for a self-publisher, book packager, book publisher, agent, or corporation, $5,000 to $50,000, plus expenses and research time. Some packagers pay a flat fee or a combination of advance and royalties. With self-publishers, charge one-fourth at the beginning of the project, one-fourth at the halfway mark, one fourth at the three-quarters point, and one-fourth upon completion. Some ghostwriters charge by thirds.
Greeting card writer	a wide range of payment, usually from $25 to $100 per card
Newsletter writer	$175 to $300 for four-page newsletter; desktop publishing charges are extra
Resume writer	$30 to $100 per resume
Speechwriter	for government officials, $4,000 for 20 minutes, plus travel expenses; for political candidates, $250+ for local candidates for 15 minutes, $375 to $800 for statewide candidates, and $1,000+ for national candidates; for business owners or executives, $80 per hour or $100 flat fee for 6 to 7 minutes and $500 to $3,000 for 30 minutes, depending on the size of the company, its budget, and the event
Writing instructor	for adult education programs, between $15 and $125 an hour, or $1,750 to $2,500 per course; for on-line programs, between $15 and $50 per student; for conference workshops, $100 to $250; for well known authors, for $2,500 or more
	If you've organized your own workshop, you will receive the full amount each attendee pays for registration—from $25 to $100 per day—minus your expenses (mailing list, room rental, refreshments, printing, postage).

FIRST-HAND ACCOUNT

Polly Starnes
Media Relations Consultant/Speechwriter

Polly Starnes has worked as an advertising copywriter for radio, TV, and print; as a technical writer; a public relations writer; and a political media relations consultant. In this first-hand account she focuses on the twelve years she spent as a speechwriter for various politicians.

She has a degree in communications from Loyola University, New Orleans, with a minor in political science.

Getting Started

"Louisiana has long had a reputation for its political climate. My family was involved in politics when I was a child. I had no interest in holding office; however, I had great fascination with the process of campaigning. The science of persuasion was a great challenge to me and represented the great power of the media.

"I once wrote a political television commercial for a gentleman who was running far, far behind the incumbent in the polls. My commercial ran only one time on the three major networks because the incumbent threatened to sue our campaign. It turned the campaign upside down. My (formerly losing) candidate won the race by a landslide. After that, I was hooked!

"Early on, I was writing copy in a radio station when a political operative came to me and asked if I was interested in taking a leave from my job for a governor's race. I was asked to write position papers, print pieces, and speeches for education and union members. I took a chance. After all, my old job would be waiting when the campaign was over.

"From there, I began to buy media for the congressman from my district and write copy for his print and electronic ads. One thing led to another and, the next thing I knew, I had networked myself into a situation where I was spending more time in Washington, D.C., than Louisiana. I moved to Washington.

"I had garnered a reputation for being able to write in a fashion that built my clients up and subtly attacked the opponents. This was a great asset in a competitive environment."

The Realities of the Work

"I worked with politicians running for office or reelection. I wrote position papers, sometimes called 'white papers,' reflecting the stand the office seeker took on a particular issue and why, how he or she would improve the situation, and how it would work to improve the lives of constituents.

"I also wrote speeches directed toward specific interests such as environmental, education, and labor unions. In addition I wrote speeches for small gatherings where a candidate would meet new people in his or her district. Sometimes, I would be the one to deliver these kinds of speeches if another gathering came up that the candidate had to attend.

"Speech and political writing is about dialogue—the dialogue of what people want to hear and how to assemble the words in a manner they understand.

"In speech writing it is important never to talk (write) down to the listener. It is equally important to be able to write and deliver a speech as though listeners know nothing about the subject, thus avoiding making them feel inadequate or ignorant. This is a fine line in speech writing.

"My clients were Democratic candidates for public office. Examples: Tony Knowles campaigned for mayor of Anchorage, Alaska, and is now the governor; former Governor Edwin Edwards; U.S. Senator Alan Cranston, campaigning for president; U.S. Representative Phil Gramm (now a senator); and former U.S. Representative Charles E. "Buddy" Roemer.

"Additionally, I wrote the speech President Ronald Reagan delivered at the initiation of the Ringling Bros. and Barnum & Bailey Circus's Safe Kids program.

"My primary speech writing was directed toward professional educators and union members. Others included any position the candidate needed to have addressed, for instance, a group would invite the candidate to speak about environmental reform or some other issue.

"If you have been with the campaign from the onset, chances are you had a hand in writing the position papers. Therefore, you would know the candidate's stance on issues (education, military issues, tax reform) and most, if not all research from that perspective would be readily available.

"The challenge can often be discovering exactly what the opposition's stand is. Research is an important factor. You also need to be a good detective—maybe even a spy (or enlist one)—so you can find out, not only what the opposition is printing in his or her position papers, but also what he or she is saying to supporters. This may entail going to public meetings where this person is speaking, and interviewing supporters for comments. By doing this, you can reach not just your client's current supporters but also the undecideds, and you can even pull people away from the other candidate through your investigation, sharp writing skills, and strategy.

"During campaign season, this is a twenty-four-hour-a-day job. You are at the campaign's and candidate's mercy. I have been called at 2:00 A.M. to write or rewrite a speech to answer some attack the opposition made during the 10:00 P.M. news. You must always be in tune with what is going on around you and listening for information about your client—whether it be at the next table in a restaurant or on the evening news.

"You must know how to listen and how act to on that information. You must also be a confidant. You must know how to ferret out information others are unable to unearth.

"You need to be flexible to work in a campaign, particularly with speech writing. You could be revising the talk as the candidate walks to the podium to speak because of a comment that was just broadcast on the news.

"You need to be a PR person when you travel with the candidate—answering questions and knowing when to say, "I don't know the answer but will get it and get back to you." And then follow through, or ensure that someone else directly from the campaign does.

"You have to be able to think quick on your feet, say the right thing, and *never* say the wrong thing.

"You must give up sleep for the campaign. You must be a fund-raiser; otherwise, one day instead of a check you will have someone come to you saying that the campaign does not have enough money to pay you this week. Make your speeches include an appeal for money at every given opportunity. You must be energetic, congenial, and never tired.

"You must be able to do anything at any time, and smile like you love every minute of it (which you probably will).

"This job, during campaign season, is nonstop. You must be able to get on an airplane at a moment's notice and think nothing of having to buy clothes when you get to your destination because you haven't been home long enough to do the laundry.

"You will have opportunities to mingle with heads of state and domestic workers—people of all ages. And, you must be able to speak their language and understand their needs.

"After the final election in November, you will have nothing to do until about March or even April. This is a good time to watch and listen to find out who the candidates will be for the next year's election. This is the time to plan a strategy to land a contract with the candidate with whom you wish to work.

"It is unwise to try to work with a candidate for money only. To write about things you do not firmly believe in will not work. Business is business, but conscience is conscience. Having tried it, I can attest that writing speeches decrying the ERA when I was a firm supporter of this movement made me angry, and I even had physical ailments from writing about something in which I did not believe. One day I took the candidate aside and said, 'You and I have been friends for a long time. Before we destroy a friendship over ideals, let's just shake hands and walk away friends.' I lost money, but I kept a friend.

"In the midst of chaos of the job, you must be the inveterate organizer. And, you must learn to delegate certain things to the right people. There is no room for error in this job. Mistakes can cost your candidate his office, reputation, and a lot of money. It can even cause the candidate and other operatives to run into legal problems."

The Upsides and Downsides

"The excitement is key to enjoyment of the job and to persuading others to believe in what you believe in.

"Time off between November and March can be good or bad. I always enjoyed it because I had a son, and during those months I was with him 100 percent. Many of my friends used this time to travel or just rest. But you must be a good money manager so you can survive these months when there is no income."

Earnings

"Each campaign is structured differently, and my fee was dependent on the size of the campaign, local or national. I usually worked on salary—from a few thousand to upward of $90,000 per campaign—depending on my direct involvement.

"I have written single speeches for $300. I have written fund-raising speeches for a percentage of what was contributed. There are as many ways to structure your fee as there are campaigns."

Advice from Polly Starnes

"You must be adaptable and willing to do anything at any time. Speechwriters might have to pitch in with a campaign, for example, and find themselves doing telephone solicitation if the volunteers don't show up.

"You need a strong interest in making the world a better place and have ideals that you would like to see met. You may have positions on certain issues that you would like to see changed, so you become involved in the campaign and grow within a network of people.

"A good place to start would be volunteering, and then going the extra mile. You will be noticed and rewarded for what you give.

"I have always believed that education is important. But, to succeed in this business, you also need talent, personality, discipline, and an insatiable curiosity for ferreting out facts to enhance your candidate.

"A good political media relations person needs to be a good PR person as well as a good writer. This is not just a writing job."

FIRST-HAND ACCOUNT

Carma Spence-Pothitt
Newsletter Writer

Carma Spence-Pothitt edits and writes the member, producer, and employer newsletters for Blue Shield of California, an HMO in San Francisco, California. She has also worked in public relations.

She has a bachelor's degree in biology from the University of California, Santa Cruz, and an M.A. in journalism from the University of Maryland, College Park.

She has been working in the field since 1993.

Getting Started

"I have always been interested in writing—I've been writing fiction and poetry since elementary school—but I also love science. So, while I was studying biology in undergraduate school I took a science writing course and fell in love with it.

"I worked for a while in customer service to save up money for graduate school, where I pursued my love of science and writing at the same time.

"Through the recommendation of my adviser, I applied for a writing position with the Maryland Agricultural Experiment Station while attending UMCP. I got the job and very much enjoyed writing about what the scientists were doing. It also looked good on my resume.

"I've gotten all my jobs in the field by sending out my resume."

The Realities of the Work

"In my particular subspecialty, publications, I take a publication—usually a newsletter, but sometimes a brochure, magazine, or flyer—from conception to printed piece. In the case of periodicals, this is an ongoing task, and often I'm working on several issues at the same time.

"I currently write eight newsletters: three that come out three times a year, four that are out four times a year, and one that is bimonthly.

"My biggest challenge is keeping my blood pressure down when others don't meet a deadline. Deadlines run what I do, and missing one not only makes one project go out late, but it affects all my other projects as well. I take a great deal of pride in the publications I produce—which explains why missing a deadline or finding a typo in a blue-line really gets to me.

"I primarily write light health care stories and business updates. The ideas are usually generated from an editorial board meeting or through material I get via E-mail that I think my audiences would find of interest. Also, sometimes my supervisor or manager mandates a story.

"In a typical day, I read and respond to a lot of E-mail, discuss potential 'fires' on the phone, and then sometimes I actually get to write! Each day is different— some days are filled with busywork, and I don't get a sense of accomplishment. Other days I'm able to write and edit a lot, and those days feel good.

"Right now, I find my job boring but that wasn't always the case. When the material I get to write is interesting to me, the job is more enjoyable.

"This job is forty-plus hours a week. It has lots of highs and lows, and depending on the specifics of your job and where you work, you can have high stress all the time, in cycles, or rarely. The more responsibility you have, the more fun and challenging the job can be, but the more stressful it can get."

The Upsides and Downsides

"I love taking the raw stuff of a publication and polishing it so that it becomes a shiny new publication. I get a lot of satisfaction from seeing a Word file turned into a newsletter or magazine.

"The most difficult aspect is dealing with people who don't respect or understand what I do. Often I can't get a project out on time because others in the company are clueless as to how a publication is created. They miss deadlines and think that's OK. They think they can change copy significantly at final review before it goes to the printer and that this can be done within twenty-four hours. They don't understand that making changes to a blue-line costs money, sometimes a lot of it."

Earnings

"When I started out I earned $20,000—which was a bummer because I was earning $25,000 before I went to graduate school to earn the degree that got me the job. But, I've slowly but surely worked my way up to around $45,000.

"Beginners should expect to start—unless they are super lucky—around the mid-twenties. With more experience, this can grow rapidly, but mainly by changing companies. Expecting raises to get you there is unrealistic."

Advice from Carma Spence-Pothitt

"Do what you love, and everything else will follow. You have to follow where your passion leads you, or you're going to be very unhappy in whatever you do, but especially in this kind of high-stress job.

"You should have communication talent—writing, speaking, interpersonal. A degree in marketing, journalism, or PR is good. And if you want to go into a specialty such as science-related material, having a degree in that area is helpful, too.

"Do what you want to do. By this I mean, if you want to be a marketing writer, volunteer your talents at a nonprofit organization to build up a portfolio of writing samples. Every time you apply for any kind of writing job, they will want to see writing samples (usually three) and it doesn't matter if you got paid to do them, just that they are good, quality work."

FINAL WORDS OF ADVICE

No matter the area of writing you choose to pursue, keep these three points in mind:

1. Be willing to work in more than one area of writing, at least until you've established yourself. Most of the professional writers who provided first-hand accounts for this book have done a variety of writing, from books to articles to newsletters to press releases. The more flexible you are, the more likely you will be able to forge a career as a writer.

2. Pay attention to your craft; hone it and polish it until it shines. Starting out, for the most part, it doesn't matter how many credits you have. Your writing will speak for itself.

3. Be persistent. Rejection is a constant companion to writers. You need to develop a thick skin and not give up. The more you improve your craft and learn the ropes of the industry, the better your chances.

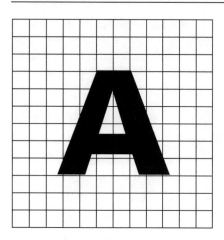

APPENDIX A: PROFESSIONAL ASSOCIATIONS

The following professional associations provide all or some of the following services: career pamphlets, newsletters, preparatory courses, market listings, agent listings, job listings, conferences, and other professional information.

AGENTS

The Association of Authors' Representatives, Inc. (AAR)
P.O. Box 237201 Ansonia Station
New York, NY 10003
Website: www.publishersweekly.com/aar/
The website contains information on working as an agent, as well as working with agents.

BOOK PUBLISHING

American Booksellers Association
Information Service Center
828 South Broadway
Tarrytown, NY 10591
E-mail: info@bookweb.org
Website: www.ambook.org/

American Society of Indexers (ASI)
P.O. Box 48267
Seattle, WA 98148
E-mail: asi@well.com
Website: www.asindexing.org/

Association of American Publishers (AAP)
50 F Street NW
Washington, DC 20001
Website: www.publishers.org/

Association of American University Presses (AAUP)
71 West 23rd Street, Suite 901
New York, NY 10010
Website: aaup.princeton.edu/

The Association of Electronic Publishers
Website: welcome.to/AEP

The Audio Publishers Association
627 Aviation Way
Manhattan Beach, CA 90266
Website: www.audiopub.org/

National Association of Independent Publishers
P.O. Box 430
Highland City, FL 33846
E-mail: NAIP@aol.com
Website: lcweb.loc.gov/loc/cfbook/coborg/nai.html

National Association of Publisher Representatives
399 East 72nd Street, Suite 3F
New York, NY 10021

Publisher's Weekly
Website: www.publishersweekly.com/

MAGAZINES

American Society of Magazine Editors
919 3rd Ave., 22 Floor
New York, NY 10022
For information on college internships in magazine editing.

Council of Literary Magazines and Presses
E-mail: CLMPNYC@aol.com
Website: www.litline.org/html/clmp.html

Magazine Publishers of America
1211 Connecticut Ave. NW
Washington, DC 20036
Website: http://publishing.about.com/business
     /publishing/msub1a.htm

Magazine Publishers Association
575 Lexington Ave.
New York, NY 10022

Society of National Association Publications
1150 Connecticut Ave. NW, Suite 1050
Washington, DC 20036
Publications owned or operated by professional associations and societies.

For magazine jobs
Website: publishing.about.com/business/publishing/msubmaga
zinejobs.htm

MARKETING, ADVERTISING, PUBLIC RELATIONS

Advertising Photographers of America, Inc.
27 West 20th Street
New York, NY 10011

Advertising Research Foundation
641 Lexington Ave.
New York, NY 10022
Annual meeting, regional meetings, workshops, and conferences.

American Advertising Federation
1101 Vermont Ave. NW, Suite 500
Washington, DC 20005

American Association of Advertising Agencies
666 3rd Ave., 13th Floor
New York, NY 10017

American Marketing Association
250 South Wacker Drive
Chicago, IL 60606
Fosters research, sponsors seminars, conferences, and student marketing clubs;
offers placement service.

Association of National Advertisers
155 East 44th Street
New York, NY 10017
Conducts studies, surveys, seminars, and workshops, and provides a specialized
education program.

Business/Professional Advertising Association
100 Metroplex Drive
Edison, NJ 08817

Graphic Communications Association
100 Daingerfield Road
Alexandria, VA 22314
Conducts tutorial programs, seminars, and workshops.

National Council for Marketing and Public Relations
c/o Becky Olson
364 North Wyndham Avenue
Greely, CO 80634
Holds an annual conference with exhibits, national surveys, needs assessment.

Point of Purchase Advertising Institute
66 North Van Brunt Street
Englewood, NJ 07631
Conducts student education programs.

Public Relations Society of America (PRSA)
33 Irving Place, 3rd Floor
New York, NY 10003
E-mail: hdq@prsa.org
Website: www.prsa.org
A comprehensive directory of schools offering degree programs or a sequence of study in public relations; a brochure on careers in public relations.

The Society for Health Care Strategy and Market Development
One North Franklin Street, Suite 3100S
Chicago, IL 60606
Public relations in hospitals and other health care settings.

Specialty Advertising Association International
3125 Skyway Circle N
Irving, TX 75038

NEWSPAPERS

Accrediting Council on Education in Journalism & Mass
     Communications
University of Kansas School of Journalism
Lawrence, KS 66045

American Newspaper Publishers Association
The Newspaper Center
11600 Sunrise Valley Drive
Reston, VA 22091

American Newspaper Publishers Association Foundation
The Newspaper Center, Box 17407
Dulles International Airport
Washington, DC 20041

American Society of Media Photographers
14 Washington Road, Suite 502
Princeton Junction, NJ 08550

American Society of Newspaper Editors
P.O. Box 4090
Reston, VA 22090

Associated Press Broadcasters Association
1825 K Street NW, Suite 710
Washington, DC 20006

Association for Education in Journalism and Mass
    Communication
University of South Carolina
LeConte College, Room 121
Columbia, SC 29208

The Dow Jones Newspaper Fund, Inc.
P.O. Box 300
Princeton, NJ 08543

Information on careers in journalism, colleges and universities offering degree programs in journalism or communications, and journalism scholarships and internships.

Investigative Reporters and Editors
100 Neff Hall
University of Missouri
Columbia, MO 65211

National Newspaper Association
1525 Wilson Blvd., Suite 550
Arlington, VA 22209

National Press Photographers Association (NPPA)
3200 Cloasdaile Drive, Suite 306
Durham, NC 27705

Newspaper Association of America
1921 Gallows Road, Suite 600
Vienna, VA 22182

Newspaper Farm Editors of America
4200 12th Street
Des Moines, IA 50313

The Newspaper Guild
Research and Information Department
8611 2nd Ave.
Silver Spring, MD 20910
Information on union wage rates for newspaper and magazine reporters.

Radio and Television News Directors Association
1717 K Street NW, Suite 615
Washington, DC 20006

WRITERS

American Association for the Advancement of Science (AAAS)
1200 New York Ave. NW
Washington, DC 20005
Website: www.aaas.org
For information on technical writing.

American Association of Agricultural Communicators of
    Tomorrow
University of Illinois
67 Mumford Hall
1301 West Gregory
Urbana, IL 61801

American Medical Writers Association (AMWA)
9650 Rockville Pike
Bethesda, Maryland 20814
E-mail: amwa@amwa.org
Website: www.amwa.org

American Society of Journalists and Authors
1501 Broadway, Suite 302
New York, NY 10036

American Translators Association (ATA)
1800 Diagonal Road, Suite 220
Alexandria, VA 22314
E-mail: 73564.2032@compuserve.com

Association for Business Communication (ABC)
Box G-1326, Baruch College
17 Lexington Ave.
New York, NY 10010
E-mail: MyersABC@compuserve.com
Website: www.theabc.org/

Association for Computing Machinery's Special Interest
    Group on Documentation (ACM/SIGDOC)
1515 Broadway, 17th Floor
New York, NY 10036
E-mail: acmhelp@acm.org
Website: www.acm.org/sigdoc/

Association for Educational Communications
    and Technology
1025 Vermont Ave. NW, Suite 820
Washington, DC 20005
Website: www.aect.org

Association for Women in Communications (AWC)
1244 Ritchie Hwy, Suite 6
Arnold, MD 21012
E-mail: womcom@aol.com

Association of Teachers of Technical Writing (ATTW)
Department of Rhetoric and Writing Studies
San Diego State University
San Diego, CA 92182
Website: rhet.agri.umn.edu/~tcq/

Authors Guild, Inc.
330 West 42nd Street
New York, NY 10036

Aviation/Space Writers' Association
17 South High Street
Columbus, OH 43215

Copywriter's Council of America
Communications Building
102 Seven Putter Lane
Middle Island, NY 11953

Council for the Advancement of Science Writing
Abbotts Building, Room 100
Philadelphia, PA 19104

Council for Programs in Technical and Scientific Communication
   (CPTSC)
New Mexico State University
English Department, Box 3E
Las Cruces, NM 88003
E-mail: sbernhar@nmsu.edu

Council of Biology Editors (CBE)
60 Revere Drive, #500
Northbrook, IL 60062
E-mail: cbehdqts@aol.com

Editorial Freelancers Association
P.O. Box 2050
Madison Square Station
New York, NY 10159

Fiction Writer's Connection (FWC)
P.O. Box 72300
Albuquerque, NM 87195
E-mail: Bcamenson@aol.com
Website: www.fictionwriters.com

Freelance Editorial Association
P.O. Box 835
Cambridge, MA 02238

Graphic Communications Association (GCA)
100 Daingerfield Road
Alexandria, VA 22314
Website: www.gca.org

Health Sciences Communications Association
6728 Old McLean Village Drive
McLean, VA 22101

Institute of Electrical and Electronics Engineers' Professional
  Communication Society (IEEE/PCS)
IEEE Operations Center, Admission and Advancement
  Department
445 Hoes Lane
P.O. Box 459
Piscataway, NJ 08855
Website: www.ieee.org/society/pcs/

IEEE Professional Communication Group
345 East 47th Street
New York, NY 10017

National Association of Agricultural Journalists
c/o Audrey Mackiewitz
312 Valley View Drive
Huron, OH 44839

National Association of Black Journalists
P.O. Box 17212
Washington, DC 20041

National Association of Government Communicators
609 South Washington Street
Alexandria, VA 22314
E-mail: info@nagc.com
Website: www.nagc.com

National Association of Hispanic Journalists
National Press Building
Washington, DC 20045

National Association of Home and Workshop Writers
c/o Alfred Lees
140 Nassau Street, Room 9B
New York, NY 10038

National Association of Science Writers
P.O. Box 294
Greenlawn, NY 11740
Website: nasw.org/

National Conference of Editorial Writers
6223 Executive Blvd.
Rockville, MD 20852

National Federation of Press Women
Box 99
Blue Springs, MO 64013

National Writer Club
2323 Troy Street
Aurora, CO 80014

National Writers Union
873 Broadway, Suite 203
New York, NY 10003

Science Fiction Writers of America
Five Winding Brook Drive, No. 18
Guilderland, NY 12084

Society of American Travel Writers
1155 Connecticut Avenue, Suite 500
Washington, DC 20006

Society for Technical Communication, Inc.
901 North Stuart Street, Suite 904
Arlington, VA 22203
Website: www.stc-va.org/

Women in Communications, Inc.
2101 Wilson Boulevard, Suite 417
Arlington, VA 22201

Writer's Alliance
Box 2014
Setauket, NY 11733

CANADIAN ASSOCIATIONS

The Association of Canadian Publishers
110 Eglinton Ave. W, Suite 401
Toronto, ON M4R 1A3
E-mail: info@canbook.org
Website: www.publishers.ca/

Canadian Authors Association
121 Avenue Road, Suite 104
Toronto, ON M5R 2G3

Canadian Publishers' Council
250 Merton Street, Suite 203
Toronto, ON M4S 1B1
E-mail: pubadmin@pubcouncil.ca
Website: www.pubcouncil.ca/

Institute of Electrical and Electronic Engineers/Professional
Communication Society (IEEE/PCS)
569 Oxford Street
Winnipeg, Manitoba R3M 3J2

Societe Quebecoise de la Redaction Professionelle (SQRP)
C.P. 126
Succursale Roxboro
Roxboro, Quebec H8Y 3ES

Writers' Alliance of Newfoundland and Labrador
P.O. Box 2681
St. John's, NF A1C 5M5

Writers' Federation of New Brunswick
P.O. Box 37, Station A
Fredericton, NB E3B 4Y2

Writers' Federation of Nova Scotia
#203, 5516 Spring Garden Road
Halifax, NS B3J 1G6

Writer's Guild of Alberta
10523 100 Ave.
Edmonton, AB T5J 0A8

Writers Union of Canada
24 Ryerson Ave.
Toronto, ON M5R 2G3

INTERNATIONAL ASSOCIATIONS

Australia Society for Technical Communication (ASTC)
68 Holmes Road
Moonee Ponds, Victoria
Australia 3039
Contact: Julie Fisher
E-mail: astc@vicnet.net.au
Website: www.vicnet.net.au/~astc

Conseil des Redacteurs Techniques (CRT)
5, Villa des Carrieres
F-94120 Fontenay-sous-Bois
France
Website: ourworld.compuserve.com/homepages/bardez_cristina

Dantekom
P.O. Box 146
DK-3600
Frederikssund
Denmark

Foreningen Teknisk Information (FTI)
Skansgatan 19
S-27231
Simrishamn
Sweden
Website: www.nts.mh.se/~fti/FTI-intr.htm

Gesellschaft fuer Technische Kommunikation (TEKOM)
Markelstrasse 34
D-70193 Stuttgart
Germany
Website: www.tekom.de

Gesellschaft fur Technische Kommunikation Schweize (TECOM
    Schweiz)
Kirchbergstrasse 30
CH-5024 Kuttigen
Switzerland

Institute of Scientific and Technical Communicators (ISTC)
Blackhorse Road
Letchworth, Herts SG6 1YY
England
Website: www.istc.org.uk

Institute of Technical Communicators in Southern Africa
(ITCSA)
Tegkom
P.O. Box 30544
0132 Sunnyside
South Africa

International Association of Audiovisual Communicators
(IAAVC)
9531 Jamacha Blvd., #263
Spring Valley, CA 91977
Website: www.cindys.com

International Association of Business Communicators (IABC)
One Hallidie Plaza, #600
San Francisco, CA 94102
Website: www.iabc.com

International Communication Association (ICA)
Box 9589
Austin, TX 78766
E-mail: icahdq@uts.cc.utexas.edu

International Council for Technical Communication
106 South Airmont Road
Suffern, NY 10901
Website: www.nts.mh.se/~fti/Intecom.htm

International Federation of Scientific Editors' Associations
c/o Dr. I. Elizabeth Zipf
Bioscience Information Service
2100 Arch Street
Philadelphia, PA 19103

International Interactive Communications Society (IICS)
10160 SW Nimbus Ave, Suite F2
Portland, OR 97223
E-mail: worldhq@iics.org
Website: www.iics.org

International Society for Performance Improvement (ISPI)
1300 L Street NW, Suite 1250
Washington, DC 20005
E-mail: info@ispi.org
Website: www.ispi.org

International Society for Technical Illustrators (ISTI)
2230 Lyndhurst Ave.
Charlotte, NC 28203

International Society for Technology in Education
University of Oregon
1781 Agate Street
Eugene, OR 97403

International Television and Video Association (ITVA)
6311 North O'Connor Road, Suite 230
Irving, TX 75039
E-mail: itvahq@worldnet.att.net
Website: www.itva.org/

International Women's Writing Guild
Box 810 Gracie Station
New York, NY 10028

Israel Society for Technical Communication (ETTY)
8 Spinoza Street, Apt. 3
Ra'anana IL-43588
Israel

Norsk Forening for Teknisk Informasjon (NFTI)
ComText AS
Gjerdrums vei 12G
N-0486 Oslo
Norway

Studiekring voor Technische Informatie and Communicatie
    (STIC)
Punselie Communication Services
St. Adrianusstr. 1
NL-5614 EL Eindhoven
The Netherlands

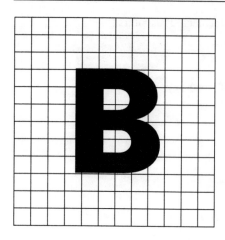

APPENDIX B: FURTHER READING

The following is a brief listing of "how-to" titles and directories that will guide you on your way to a career in writing.

COPYEDITING

The Chicago Manual of Style, Chicago, IL: University of Chicago Press.

FICTION

Your Novel Proposal: From Creation to Contract, by Blythe Camenson and Marshall J. Cook (Writer's Digest Books).

MARKETING, ADVERTISING, PUBLIC RELATIONS

Great Jobs for Communications Majors, by Blythe Camenson (VGM Career Books).

> *Advertising Career Directory*
> Public Relations Career Directory
> Gale Research, Inc.
> P.O. Box 33477
> Detroit, MI 48232

> *Standard Directory of Advertising Agencies*
> Reed Reference Publishing
> P.O. Box 31
> New Providence, NJ 07974

Known as the *Agency Red Book*, it lists over 4,000 agencies and includes regional offices, accounts specializations, number of employees, and names and titles of key personnel. It is published every February, June, and October.

NONFICTION

How to Write a Book Proposal, by Michael Larsen (Writer's Digest Books).
How to Write Irresistible Query Letters, by Lisa Collier Cool (Writer's Digest Books).
Technical Writer's Freelancing Guide, by Peter Kent (Sterling).

> *Magazine Publishing Career Directory*
> Gale Research, Inc.
> P.O. Box 33477
> Detroit, MI 48232

YOUNG WRITERS

Career Portraits: Writing, by Blythe Camenson (VGM Career Books).

MARKET GUIDES

Guide to Literary Agents (Writer's Digest Books).
Market Guide for Young Writers (Writer's Digest Books).
Novel and Short Story Writer's Market (Writer's Digest Books).
Photographer's Market (Writer's Digest Books).
Poet's Market (Writer's Digest Books).
Writer's Market (Writer's Digest Books).

> *The International Directory of Little Magazines and Small Presses*
> Dustbooks
> Box 100
> Paradise, CA 95967

> *Writer's Digest Magazine*
> P.O. Box 2124
> Harlan, IA 51593

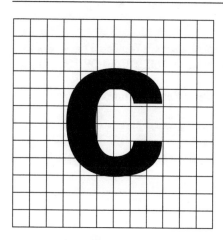

APPENDIX C: PREPARATORY PROGRAMS FOR WRITING FIELDS

The following is a sampling of the many institutions that offer courses and programs in the different areas of the writing field. To locate current addresses, phone numbers, and websites, do an Internet search or refer to any of the college directories, available in public libraries.

Arizona State University
Creative Writing Program

Arkansas State University
Printing Program

Association of Graphic Communications
Graphic Arts Education Center

Baylor University
Writing Program

Binghamton University
Writing Program

Boston University
Graduate Creative Writing Program

Bowling Green State University
Creative Writing Program

Center for Book Arts
Bookbinding, printing, and papermaking workshops

Chicago Book Clinic Seminars
Seminars for publishers

Childworks Agency
White Pines National Conference for Writers and Illustrators of Children's
Books

Columbia University School of the Arts
Writing Division

Dynamic Graphics Educational Foundation
Professional workshops and seminars

Emerson College
Writing and Publishing Program

Fiction Writer's Connection
Writing for Publication E-mail Course Program

Fordham University
Graduate School of Business Administration

George Washington University
Center for Career Education

Graphic Arts Guild New York
Business workshops and seminars

H. H. Herbert School of Journalism & Mass Communication
Professional Writing Program

Hamilton College
English/Creative Writing

Harvard University
Radcliffe Publishing Course

Hofstra University
English Department

Hollins College
Writing Program

Louisiana State University
Writing Program

Massachusetts College of Art
Writing Children's Literature

McNeese State University
Writing Program

Mississippi Review/University of Southern Mississippi
Center for Writers

Mystery Writers of America Inc.
Writing Workshops

The National Writer's Voice Project
The Writer's Voice of New York, New York

New York City Technical College
Center for Advertising, Printing and Publishing

New York University
Center for Publishing

Oberlin College
Creative Writing Program

Ohio University
English Department, Creative Writing Program

Pace University
Master of Science in Publishing

Parsons School of Design
Design courses

Rice University Continuing Studies
Rice University Publishing Program

Rochester Institute of Technology
School of Printing

School of Visual Arts
New York

Stanford University
Stanford Professional Publishing Course

Syracuse University
Creative Writing Program and
S.I. Newhouse School of Public Communications

University of Alabama
Program in Creative Writing

University of Baltimore—Yale Gordon College of Liberal Arts
Institute for Language, Technology and Publications Design

University of California Extension
Certificate Program in Publishing and Professional Sequence in
Copyediting

University of Chicago
Graham School of General Studies

The University of Connecticut
The Realities of Publishing

University of Denver
Publishing Institute

University of Hawaii
Manoa Writing Program

University of Houston
Creative Writing Program

University of Illinois at Chicago
Program for Writers

University of Illinois
Department of Journalism

University of Iowa
Writer's Workshop, Graduate Creative Writing Program

University of Missouri—Kansas City
New Letters Weekend Writers Conference

University of Montana
Environmental Writing Institute

University of Pennsylvania
College of General Studies Special Programs

University of Southern California
Professional Writing Program

University of Texas at Austin
Writing Program

University of Texas at El Paso
Writing Program

University of Virginia
Publishing and Communications Program

University of Wisconsin
Madison Communication Programs

Vermont College
MFA Writing Program

Warren Wilson College
MFA Program for Writers

Washington University
The Writing Program

Writer's Digest School
Correspondence courses

For a list of schools with accredited programs in journalism and public relations, send a stamped, self-addressed envelope to:

> Accrediting Council on Education in Journalism and Mass
>   Communications
> University of Kansas School of Journalism
> Stauffer-Flint Hall
> Lawrence, KS 66045

Names and locations of newspapers and a list of schools and departments of journalism are published in the *Editor and Publisher International Year Book*, available in public libraries.

DATE DUE